# In Charge

# In Charge

## *Supervising for the First Time*

■

GORDON P. RABEY

the Institute
of Management

PITMAN PUBLISHING

PITMAN PUBLISHING
128 Long Acre, London WC2E 9AN

A Division of Longman Group UK Limited

First published in Great Britain 1994

**British Library Cataloguing in Publication Data**
A CIP catalogue record for this book can be obtained
from the British Library.

ISBN 0 273 60426 0 (Paper back)
ISBN 0 273 60750 2 (Cased)

Printed and bound in Great Britain
by Bell and Bain Ltd, Glasgow

*The Publisher's policy is to use paper manufactured from sustainable forests.*

To Paula

With thanks to Ern Prentice of General Motors-Holdens
for his continuing support.

# CONTENTS

# PREFACE

Mainly for the managers to whom supervisors and frontline managers report.

## SETTING THE SCENE

### The Supervisors' World

The traditional world of the supervisor as the unit boss who gives directions, the autocratic in-charge person who must be obeyed, has disappeared. It has little relevance in today's work place. Results are still the reality, but organisations are now realising that unless all employees believe in the work objectives and are committed to their achievement management's expectations are not likely to be met.

New practices of supervision and of management have evolved and the learning curve is not diminishing. The mind map which follows was the response to the question 'What are the targets of focus in today's successful organisations?'

Ten headings emerged, not in a particular sequence, but all were held to be essential

(a) Work output which meets standards of quantity, quality, cost and time, and which maintains financial viability
(b) Technical competence, today and tomorrow
(c) Customer focus, in-house and external
(d) Continuous improvement to achieve better with less
(e) Effective communication and feedback processes
(f) Leadership and teamwork
(g) Competency in interpersonal relationships
(h) Problem-solving skills
(i) Coordination of activities
(j) Adherence to legislative requirements.

In each the supervisor is a key player whose effectiveness will significantly affect the outcomes.

But the identification of the ingredients for success does not tell the full story, nor does it offer ready made solutions. Much then depends upon

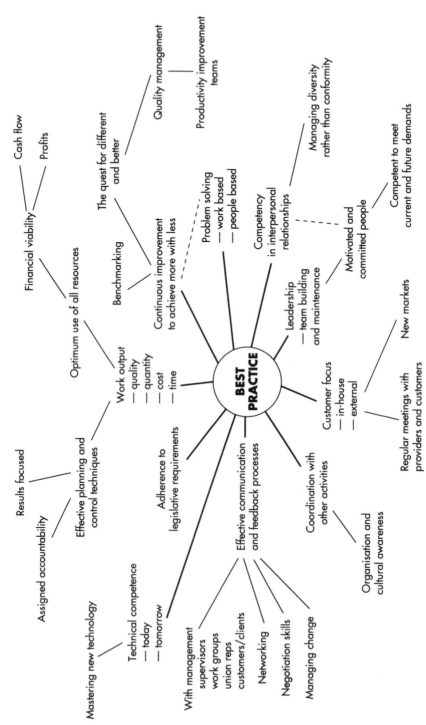

Cash flow
Profits
Financial viability
Quality management
Productivity improvement teams
The quest for different and better
Managing diversity rather than conformity
Optimum use of all resources
Benchmarking
Problem solving
— work based
— people based
Continuous improvement to achieve more with less
Competency in interpersonal relationships
Competent to meet current and future demands
Work output
— quality
— quantity
— cost
— time
Motivated and committed people
Results focused
Effective planning and control techniques
Leadership
— team building and maintenance

**BEST PRACTICE**

Assigned accountability
Adherence to legislative requirements
Customer focus
— in-house
— external
New markets
Mastering new technology
Technical competence
— today
— tomorrow
Effective communication and feedback processes
Coordination with other activities
Regular meetings with providers and customers
With management
supervisors
work groups
union reps
customers/clients
Networking
Negotiation skills
Managing change
Organisation and cultural awareness

**The focus of effective organisations**

the mix of those ingredients and upon the recipes in which they are brought together.

Research studies in several countries looking at the outputs of companies working in identical situations and with comparable labour pools, where productivity showed striking variations, concluded that the primary difference was the way in which management worked with the employees. The most productive operations were those where employees had significantly more individual responsibility and involvement in goal setting and in problem solving.

In theory this should give a clear guideline for action, but the reality shows some of the hurdles which first must be overcome. Most enterprises have been through, and in many cases are still going through, restructuring and reorganising which has inevitably led to staffing reductions ('downsizing' or 'rightsizing', to quote the jargon).

The ranks of middle managers have been reduced drastically, an increasing volume of work is being put out on contract or being assigned to temporary workers, there is an unremitting quest to accomplish better with less, competition is becoming fiercer, and many managers are being driven by crisis deadlines rather than by rational planning.

In this frenetic environment supervisors are emerging as an organisation's key resource, for they control the people who do the work, who have the customer contact, and whose performance ultimately determines success or failure, profit or loss.

Supervisors working with limited resources of skill, finance, time, and uncertainty of tenure are now facing quick fix demands for

**Work Place Reform** which encompasses participative

Quality management which is cost-effective

Market driven activity and customer focus

Continuous improvement

Higher profit with less input

Performance measurement

Coping with and managing new technology

Managing diversity rather than conformity

Work-based learning

Leading change

Conversion to a team leadership role

Effective control and coping skills

for which many supervisors are quite inadequately prepared.

Now there are strident calls for better and more comprehensive training of supervisors and for national certification of their competency. Considerable effort and finance is being directed to this end.

No doubt this will achieve much but it should be seen only as a partial solution. Work flows between functions and across levels of authority and singling out one group for special attention will not produce the desired outcomes. There have been so many perceived remedies for organisational defects: the drives for management by objectives, excellence, alphabetical theories, quality circles, performance management, competency identification, leadership and team work, total quality management, managing diversity, and the quest continues. Each has its value, indeed some can claim very significant achievements, but after some eighteen months of high profile a new guru usually appears whose nostrum attracts new devotees. Someone has said it's time we got back to steering by the stars instead of by the lights of passing ships.

An organisation is a whole being living within its own culture and with its own in-built defence mechanisms. It must maintain its own health and develop its own strategies for coping with its environment. To do this it will draw on many resources, particularly on those listed above which have demonstrated real effectiveness, but the continuing strength must come from the coordinated and supportive actions of the management group, which must include its supervisors.

This book centres on the tools and techniques of *Supervisory Practice*, but it must be stressed that the contribution of supervisors to organisational productivity will be dependent upon their place in the management partnership and upon the mentoring and support they receive in this relationship.

## Supervisors are your Primary Resource

The present economic climate makes return on investment a vital factor both in the private and the public sectors of business activity.

Costs must be held — and reduced if at all possible. Productivity and operational effectiveness must be increased.

**Better productivity comes from people working competently together towards an objective to which they are committed.**

The people at the sharp end, the employees, are usually the ones who produce the goods or provide the services, and they react to the stimulus and the example of their immediate bosses, their supervisors or front line managers. To a high degree it is within the hands of supervisors whether or not objectives are reached within budgets.

Supervisors are key people.

They can significantly affect productivity and effectiveness and thereby your profitability.

They can control your shop window — whether this be a service area, a public counter or a telephone contact — and your most negative and potent public relations impact comes from dissatisfied customers or clients.

They influence morale and motivation.

They are the link between management and staff.

**Your supervisors and front line managers are your most important resource.**

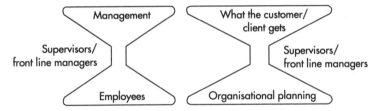

Supervisors occupy the pivotal position between the planning and the doing.

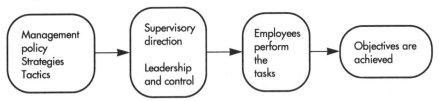

The role of the supervisor today is changing. This is due to

- An awareness of the power of the worker and that if there is to be loyalty to the employing organisation this loyalty must be earned
- The trend towards the flattening of the hierarchical pyramid by reducing the layers of middle management
- The logical direct communication which must grow between the desk top computers of senior management and the action level of the work force
- The emergence of a better educated work force and the social awareness of their right to be consulted
- A growing realisation that people at the work place to take an interest in their work and want to know what is happening
- An increasing concern of how costly it can be if a supervisor fails.

**The performance of your supervisors makes your reputation.**

Within their areas of activity each supervisor can be expected to be a

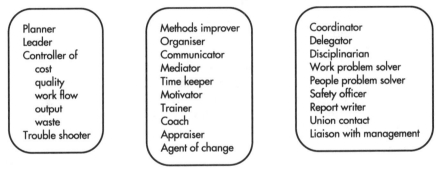

and more roles can be added as appropriate. Supervisors are expected from the date of their appointment to be competent in each. Their performance is appraised as such.

Four questions must emerge here

1 Who trained them to perform each of these roles and how well was this done?
2 In addition to these roles many have personal work assignments — they too are workers — do they really have time and opportunity to supervise adequately?
3 Does their pay level recognise this responsibility compared with the people they supervise?
4 How well informed are they?

In times of industrial relations sensitivity management becomes increasingly concerned with the need for better communication with unions. They seek to keep the union representatives and the delegates informed regarding both the intent and the content of their planning. And within the union the communication network is usually very effective.

Yet supervisors are seldom involved in any of these management-union discussions. Later they may be told the content of matters considered to be important but they still may not know the background intent.

**If the union delegate is a better and more detailed source of information than the supervisor who really leads the work group?**

How well will your objectives be achieved?


## ARE YOUR SUPERVISORS MEMBERS OF YOUR MANAGEMENT TEAM? — CONSULTED BY MANAGEMENT AND AWARE OF MANAGEMENT DECISIONS?

How do your supervisors see this?

Some 2600 supervisors across a very wide spectrum of organisations in both the private and public sectors were asked:

'Where you work do you feel you are part of the management team?'

6 per cent said 'yes'

21 per cent said 'sometimes'

73 per cent said 'no way' (and that's 1898 supervisors).

And of these 1898 some 9 per cent (171) stated they did not want to be supervisors, the job gave them no satisfaction.

If you personally were responsible for the performance of a piece of equipment worth, say, $400 000 how much time would you spend checking on this each week?

How much is a good supervisor worth?

How much time does a manager spend talking with and listening to each supervisor each week — discussing work in progress and projected, considering problems and solutions, and in acting as a coach to these team members? Would, for instance, 30 minutes with each (1.25 per cent of a 40-hour week) be a reasonable objective? Recognising, of course, that to do this the manager may need to do some personal time management.

**Supervisors and front line managers are key people in any organisation but they can be fully effective only as informed and trusted members of the management team.**

The competent supervisor must
- clearly understand the job
- know exactly what is required
- be trained to achieve results
- be kept informed on current and future action and feel part of the management team.

**If you improve the quality of supervision productivity and effectiveness will increase.**

It will be noted that the words 'Human Resource Management' and 'Human Resource Development' do not appear. They conjure up a picture of a material commodity which can be manipulated or positioned to achieve some predetermined objective. The phrases seem cold and clinical, to be applied to subordinates — never to ourselves.

# INTRODUCTION

No doubt you will have read the last few pages addressed to your manager — the person to whom you report. These are important and you should make sure that he or she has read them too. In your job, if you are to be really effective, and that's what you are being paid for, it is essential that you and your manager are working together in harmony towards common objectives.

Being a supervisor or a front line manager is not easy. Being an effective supervisor means a lot of work to master the necessary knowledge and skills.

A new supervisor needs plenty of help. You, like others before you, may have been told 'you're now a supervisor. You're now in charge. You'll soon pick up what is required, and if it can be arranged we hope to send you to a training course sometime soon. The best of luck'.

Then in the weeks that follow you learn that you are now being judged not on what you do, no matter how hard you work, but on what your unit does, and that this unit is looking to you for planning, for organising, for leadership, for control and for communication. And they will respond to your example.

This guide has been written to help you to handle some of the challenges you will meet in your new position where you must now achieve objectives through your leadership.

Supervisors are required to be effective — if they are not they are not supervisors.

Gordon P Rabey
Wellington, New Zealand

# PART 1

# YOU AND YOUR JOB

# CHAPTER 1

# THE EFFECTS OF NEW ORGANISATIONAL CONCEPTS

Traditionally an organisation has been seen as a pyramid — from senior executives down through a hierarchy of roles to the bottom level of employees. No other possibilities were considered, the original model being the army.

More recently, as the economic realities of international competitiveness began to threaten organisational survival, as the realisation of the constructive and creative potential of people became more evident, this pyramidal shape came under challenge. As bottom line results were seen to be the only criterion for existence it was apparent that each level of management would have to justify its status by adding value to the outputs of product or service, and the predominantly monitoring or advisory roles would no longer suffice.

So the 'flattening of the pyramid' began, layers of middle management disappeared, the role of supervisors became more important, and new reward systems had to be devised.

Further change followed. Restructuring required reorganising, there was increasing demand to achieve better with less, which led to reductions of staff numbers. New words were created — 'downsizing', 'rightsizing' — and job tenure was no longer a certainty.

There was increased decentralisation of activity and decision making, facilitated by improved communication processes and driven by an urge to get closer to the customers. But than this was offset to a degree by a centralisation of control which would enable a rapid response to the actions of competitors or other national or international events.

This led in larger organisations to the establishment of functional or regional business units operating autonomously under policy directions from a corporate head office. They were required to survive by their own efforts.

Then came the awareness, obvious with hindsight, that every organisation exists only to meet the needs of its customers or clients — the requirement to be market driven rather than product driven. The necessity for emphasis on quality was given top priority. This generated a new look at the pyramid structure and the conclusion that more properly it should be reversed:

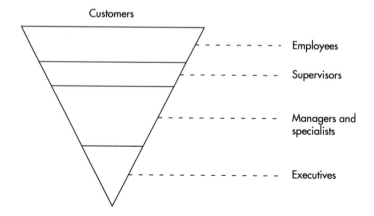

This highlighted the vital role of the supervisors — the people who plan, allocate and control the work and the output of those who supply product or service to customers.

And, perhaps for the first time, it made the point that a key responsibility of all other senior positions is to support and empower these supervisors.

The supervisor's job had changed, radically, and now requires higher standards of competency across a wider spectrum of activities.

But the factors which led to these structural realignments are only the framework to support the operational strategies which have changed the ways by which business is currently conducted. Many organisations now work to a sequence of

- A statement of vision, policy and direction
- The identification of the factors essential for goal success
- Structuring the processes necessary to achieve these success factors
- Setting measurable and timeset objectives for each stage of the processes
- Sharing these with and gaining the commitment of employees to their achievement
- Establishing explicit standards for each stage of the processes so that progress may be measured or assessed and that performance may be monitored
- Assigning individual accountabilities for performance outcomes.

Each of these can be redefined at the action level in terms of the supervisory function, and each will require the acquisition and the application of appropriate knowledge, skills and behaviour.

# CHAPTER 2

# THE DIMENSIONS OF YOUR JOB

Management internationally is now recognising that if organisations are to be effective there must be

- Clear direction and focus
- Insistence on total quality management
- Assignment of individual accountability at all levels
- Realisation that unless people are operating as motivated and committed teams organisational objectives will probably not be achieved
- Continuous improvement
- Development of multi-skilled people
- Belief that success is the business of establishing and maintaining confidence.

This has direct relevance to your organisation and to your job.

You have been put in charge. You have been promoted because management saw your potential and the value of your work and felt that you could now take charge of one of the operations. Your new title might be manager, unit head, charge hand, leading hand, team leader, foreman, supervisor or something else, but in this guide we will use the term supervisor. This means that in your new position you are now responsible and have authority for planning and controlling the work of a number of people — your unit or group — and for achieving the objectives set by management.

Until now:

But as a supervisor your task has changed. Now:

You must now demonstrate new skills, new knowledge and new behaviours.

You are no longer being paid to do the job yourself, but to ensure that it is done as required. But though your objective is clear and you are keen to achieve results it may not be so clear to the individuals in your work group and they may not share your feeling of commitment or your sense of purpose.

So if you are to be effective you must succeed as a leader who people follow because they choose to.

Right at the start, both you and the person you report to — your manager — must understand clearly what and who you are in charge of and what authority you really have.

Your **responsibilities** are those things you must do and which you must account for, and the results you should produce. This includes not only production or work performance, but can also cover such things as stock control, hiring people, quality standards and running a risk-free operation.

Your **authority** is the power which the manager has given you to carry out your responsibilities — how much stock you can order without having to get permission, how much money you can spend, how much control you can exercise, and so on.

Unless you have the authority to do the things you are responsible for you will not be able to function effectively — and you can't really be held responsible.

But this doesn't apply to every position in the organisation. Management sometimes appoints specialists to help operational people like you — perhaps a safety officer, a training officer, or someone on management services — and these specialists have responsibility but no approval authority. They can make recommendations but they cannot give direct instructions to you or to your employees. Line people carry profit and loss responsibility.

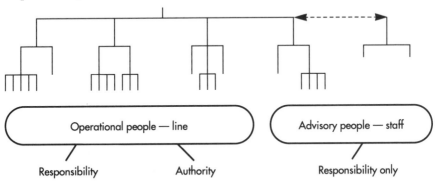

Staff people must be watched. Because they have no authority their work can be frustrating if line management does not give quick and positive attention to their recommendations. They have no power base and sometimes they will seek to establish one which takes them beyond their approved terms of reference and to intervene in operational activity. Committees of various kinds set up by management are also limited to a recommendatory role unless they have defined executive authority. They too should be watched.

But for every person — both line and staff — there should be another factor: **accountability**. This means liability for performance, for meeting the expected output requirements of the job, for producing results (which is not the same as being busy). People are employed solely to get work done and if the organisation is to get an adequate return on its investment in salaries and wages there must be a continuing evaluation of performance. This is discussed further when Job Descriptions are considered.

Without personal accountability at all levels any policy or programme will probably fail

Accountability is assigned to an individual, not to a group.

Responsibilities and authority vary tremendously in different organisations, but overall you must be responsible for

- Planning

  the work and deciding how, when and where it can best be done and by whom
- Organising

  your resources — people, time, money, equipment or material — so that jobs will be finished on time. This includes assigning work to people
- Leading

  and coaching the people in your work unit so that they work together to the best of their abilities and work as a team to achieve agreed objectives
- Controlling and performance measurement

  all things needed for the work to go well, such as production, work flow and output, quality standards, costs, waste or spoilage, machine maintenance, the training of people and for operating within budgets
- Communicating

  so that everyone who needs to know does know not only what is happening but also what is likely to happen — the manager, other supervisors, the people in the group, and perhaps technical staff or shop stewards, and others.

**These are the criteria of your effectiveness.** As a leader of a work team you must be concerned not only with the management of work and with the management of people but predominantly with the management of people's work so that targets are reached.

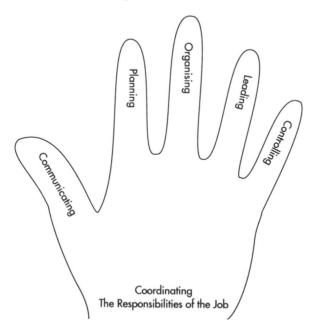

Coordinating
The Responsibilities of the Job

The hand of the supervisor
— your tools for doing the job

The precise nature of your tasks will vary according to the type of work you do and the organisation for which you work but in many instances the role of the supervisor today is changing markedly. In some situations, supervisors are now responsible for

- Selecting and appointing employees
- On job training and coaching
- Communicating all matters on a face to face basis (a 5-minute meeting at the start of each day)
- Maintaining a customer focus
- Total responsibility for quality
- Preparation of work rosters
- Continuous improvement in all aspects of work performance and output (the Japanese call this 'kaizen')
- Leading their group in problem solving
- Basic maintenance (in association with maintenance staff)
- All relevant paper work and reporting
- High levels of attendance and timekeeping.

One standard definition of a supervisor's job used to be

**To lead your team to produce work of high quality and high quantity at an economic cost within a defined time and in an atmosphere of high morale.**

This is still true but the position is now being extended both in range and depth and the level of supervisory skills and knowledge required is higher than ever before.

In addition to the performance of assigned duties you should know and understand such things as

- The overall direction of the organisation and where the work of your unit fits into this
- The culture of the organisation
- Where your priorities lie
- Policies, rules and regulations concerned with your job
- The financial expectations from your unit
- The constraints under which you must operate
- The operational requirements of the job and the output standards
- The costing or the payment procedures
- The control methods applying to your activities
- Terms of the agreement in force between your organisation and the union
- How to introduce new employees into your work group
- How to train and re-train in work skills, and how to coach
- How to deal with grievances or complaints

- How to discipline employees
- How to prevent accidents and maintain a safe working environment
- How to coordinate and co-operate with other work units
- How to work with shop stewards or union representatives.

Yours is a most important job and you are responsible to several people for different things.

You must fill many roles in the performance of your tasks and each must be done competently.

To your employees you represent management, and to management you are the link with the employees. Yet you must speak and act with the authority of your own position. Much of your success as a supervisor will depend on how well you do this.

**Your relationships:**

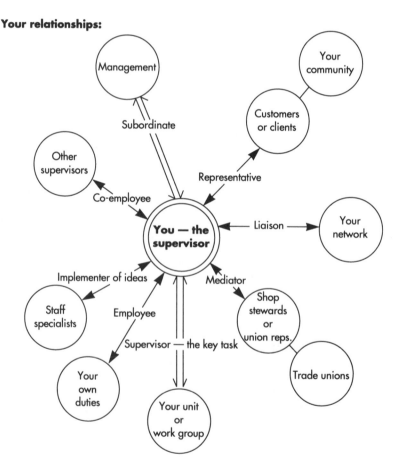

**Your management will expect**

- Group output to quality standards
- Achievement of targets within budgets
- High morale and commitment
- Loyalty (fair interpretation of management thinking)
- Advice and warning of likely events
- Waste control (time, cost, space, power, materials)
- Problem solving and creative thinking
- Focus on customers

**The people working for you will expect**

- Clear direction and objectives, including target dates
- To know the required performance standards
- Equal and fair treatment
- Good training and coaching on their present work to prepare them for advancement
- Feedback on performance
- Proper equipment and adequate resources
- Good working conditions
- An even work flow free from peaks and troughs
- Recognition of their performance and of their worth as individuals
- To develop as a team
- Encouragement of effort
- Protection from hazards
- A good example
- Information on what is happening and on what is going to happen

**Other supervisors will expect**

- Co-operation
- Your part of the total task to be done well and on time
- Maintenance of standards

But here there is a hidden but very real difficulty. **Supervision, done properly, will take time.** Yet you are expected also to do work and you probably feel that as an employee you have to set an example to your group. But you are now being paid — and judged — as a supervisor and it is on the development of these skills that your further promotion depends.

Look at it this way:

Your work group

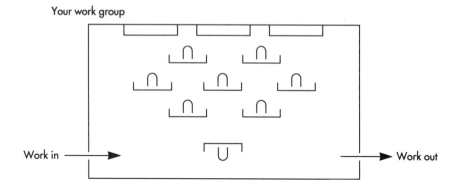

People do the work for which they are employed but this requires

- A planned work flow and control
- The competency of people to do it
- The motivation of people to do it well
- The provision of adequate resources.

However, what happens

- If one work station stops?
- If work comes back?
- If performance misses targets?
- If the work flow is erratic?
- If a crisis hits?
- If you have a problem employee?

And to this must be added your interactive responsibilities with other groups.

You can see now why you were appointed.

## MANAGING YOUR PRIORITIES

You may feel at this point like a juggler who is expected to control simultaneously a number of balls — but you do not have to do all things simultaneously. **Your strength will lie in your ability to manage your priorities**. There will be conflicting demands on your time and you have to make conscious choices about which to do first.

Move quietly and thoughtfully until you have gained the confidence that comes with competence. Remember that some people grow with responsibility, others only swell.

12

There are five major areas of your responsibility and within each there can be other conflicts of need. Your primary task is to get work done which will achieve objectives and with this constantly in mind you must then assess your other priorities by the circumstances of the situation and the effects of their impact.

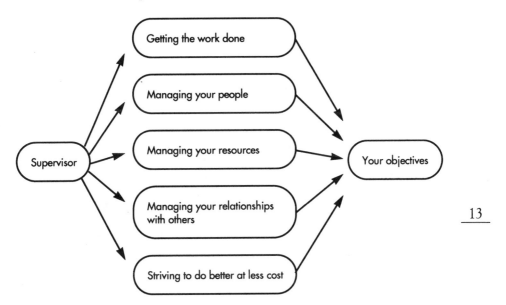

13

## THE NATURE OF YOUR ORGANISATION

The unit or group of which you are now in charge may be a key part of a small business, perhaps reporting to one manager, and it might seem that consideration of how an organisation works is not really relevant to what you do. But it is. As you read on you will realise that the points made apply to every organisation, both small and large.

There are levels of employees through to management — a hierarchy — but an organisation is not a structure of assigned roles.

It is a network of relationships between people working together for a common purpose, and as such it is not static, it is dynamic. The achievements of an organisation are the results of the combined efforts of each individual in it.

The organisation chart will tell you quite a lot about

- functions and titles
- lines of responsibility
- the span of control (how many people report directly to one supervisor or to one manager)
- the formal communication network

but it will not tell you

- whether the organisation is competent
- what really happens
- who has power and influence (the informal organisation).

Just as an individual has hidden depths of personality, of behaviour, so does an organisation.

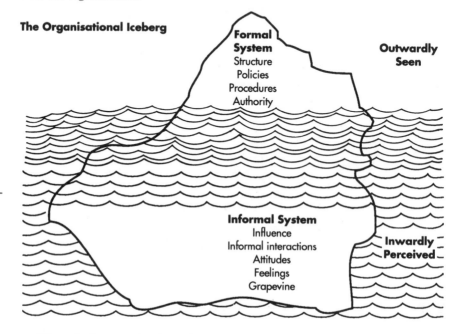

**The Organisational Iceberg**

**Formal System**
Structure
Policies
Procedures
Authority

**Outwardly Seen**

**Informal System**
Influence
Informal interactions
Attitudes
Feelings
Grapevine

**Inwardly Perceived**

Though there is the formal organisation structure which can be shown on an organisation chart (or family tree) which defines the area of authority, and which shows the line (operational) and the staff (advisory) functions, there is always an informal organisation, or area of influence, operating inside it.

This informal organisation recognises that the power and influence of some people can stem either from their personalities or from their technical skills rather than from their work positions or titles, and frequently the group will respond more to them than to a formal authority. Informal leadership can change in different situations and communication is usually maintained through the grapevine.

**Culture** is the key element of the informal organisation. It has been defined as the visible outcome of actions or behaviours within an organisation or a group which by repetition have become habitual, and which are now a set of unwritten rules and values by which people should behave in that environment. It is often a reflection of the leadership style: people oriented or task oriented, conservative or innovative, by-the-book or situational, autocratic or participative, fast acting or reflective, centralised or decentralised. When something goes wrong do people ask 'who?' or 'what?' Who has power and how is it used? What gets rewarded?

Outside their work units people are linked only by the functional interdependence of common goals and by the commonality of the organisation's culture and values.

With experience you can change the culture within your own unit, but on the wider front it is essential that you understand the organisational culture for your effectiveness will depend upon how well you are able to operate within it.

When you make recommendations or seek to introduce change you must be aware of both the formal and informal systems. You must know where power really lies, whose support is essential to your success and who can foul up what you are trying to do. This understanding of organisational politics is essential.

The task of administration is to make the organisation work.

15

An organisation to be effective must have rules and hopefully these are applied intelligently. But they must be reviewed regularly to ensure that they are still relevant and necessary. However, you should never overlook the **law of the situation**, because this is critical. It asks, 'What does this situation at this time in this place with this person require?' And that will indicate what ought to be done, and it may override the established procedures.

Your own role in the organisation is not simply to fill a position on the chart. It should evolve through three stages

1 Learning the 'rules of the game' to acquire the knowledge and skills of supervision and front line management, how to deal with the many and varied demands of the job.
2 Leading your unit, as a team leader, to achieve objectives, to develop the skills of people, to meet budget, to reduce costs, and to meet the functional requirements of the unit.

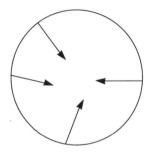

3   Maintaining a continuous liaison with other units and with customers. Tasks are not confined within units — they are cross-functional — and supervisors need to have regular communication with the sources (the providers) of their tasks and with those to whom the product or service passes (the customers).

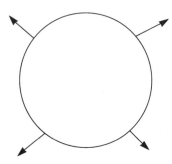

Which other units can influence your success?
How good is your relationship with them?

Traditionally organisations have worked in a linear pattern — a series of sequential steps, rather like passing the baton in a relay race. The approach today is for team work, coordinating activities so that all units are informed about current and projected activities and communication channels are unblocked.

## JOB DESCRIPTIONS AND ACCOUNTABILITY

Every person in your organisation

- Should have a job or a parcel of jobs for which he or she will be personally responsible
- Has a right to know the boundaries of that job. But because you cannot anticipate every eventuality and because there will always be one-off jobs every assignment of duties must include the clause 'and such other duties as may from time to time be required in this position'. The omission of this can lead to demarcation arguments
- Has a right to know the standards by which performance will be judged. If one of your people is not performing to the standard you expect both of you must know what that standard is. The question 'compared with what?' must be answered clearly, otherwise the issue will become one of personality confrontation rather than one of an objective work analysis.

Each of us wants continuing reassurance on two points
  'Tell me what you expect of me.'
  'Tell me how am I getting on.'
  and the Job Description should provide the source for this.

The need for clear definition here becomes critical if you find yourself in a situation where poor performance of an employee could lead into disciplinary action. If effective action is to be taken the evidence must be documented and this can only be on the basis of a defined and accepted standard. Furthermore, when an employee knows this standard a measure for self-assessment has been established and the need for close supervision can be reduced.

Your own position should be covered by a **Job Description** which meets these criteria. One example is:

| **Job title:** | | |
|---|---|---|
| The primary purpose of this position is: | | |
| Who I am responsible to: | | |
| Who is responsible to me: | | |
| Who else I have responsibilities to: | | |
| My key tasks are | I have authority to | I am effective if |
| | | |
| What special reports or other actions are required and how often: | | |

And here the final column, the performance standard, would be discussed and agreed between your manager and yourself, not imposed. This describes your accountabilities.

From this it will be seen that an evaluation of the defined work output is in effect a continuing performance appraisal.

Conditions change in most jobs, so you and your manager should review your Job Description every three months to ensure that it is still correct. This will mean that you will know quite clearly what your job is and how well you are doing it. Similar action should be taken with your subordinates and their Job Descriptions.

You should ensure that your responsibilities for contacts with other people and other groups are identified. It sometimes happens that those contacts are more important than some of your listed tasks and they will require both communicating and negotiating skills. These are called interactive skills.

Job Descriptions must be helpful and flexible — they should be facilitating not restrictive. And if a group of your employees is doing identical tasks, there is value in preparing a Group Job Description and then in using this, say, once monthly for a group performance appraisal discusssion led by yourself.

## KEY FACTORS FOR SUCCESS (KFS)

Generally you have little control over what happens to you, but you have full control over how you react to it.

---

Some of the qualities which will determine your success are

- Vision, direction and focus
- The power of analysis
- Creative imagination
- A sense of reality
- A helicopter ability to stand back and see the job objectively
- Effective leadership
- Good interactive relationships
- A concern for results and ability to achieve them
- An understanding of how the organisation works
- An ability to analyse and to resolve problems
- Good time management
- An ability to use resources effectively.

To which must be added the special technical knowledge and skills required in your own particular job.

A continuing pressure on all supervisors — sometimes, it may seem, to the exclusion of everything else — is the demand to solve the daily problems. This firefighting is always reactive, the problem is there and you have to deal with it, quickly. You seldom have time to 'walk the job' and look wider to seek and find the causes of your frequent problems and to take preventive action. But you should.

In the midst of the urgency for the quick fix, which dominates much of today's organisational activity, the longer term needs tend to be put to one side.

Your work performance is building your personal reputation. You must identify the key factors for your success, examine them regularly, and ensure that none is being overlooked.

## THE SOURCE OF POWER

Power is the ability to influence and to control others. Leadership is the exercise of power. 'Power' is not a negative word.

Power can be assigned to, or conferred on, people through job title or status, or it may be assumed through technical skill, strength of personality, or demonstrated through group behaviour.

Supervisors, and managers, are dependent on the activities of a variety of other people. Management has the power to issue instructions to employees to perform tasks which meet required standards, but the employees individually and collectively have the power to determine their input of diligence, enthusiasm, and concern for quality, cost and innovation. Employees if they so choose can exercise significant power.

So, to meet the demands of their accountabilities supervisors must develop appropriate countervailing power.

> In your position who are you dependent on?
> For what? Does this pose problems? Why?

As a supervisor you have power through the authority of your position but this must be reinforced by other behaviours for by itself it will not suffice. You will need

- The authority of knowledge, not only in the context of personal competencies but also by building an information base on everything relating to the work of your unit and of the organisation
- The authority of skill in your interpersonal relationships
  — with managers, fellow supervisors, and the customers of your unit, so that you build a reputation for helpfulness and co-operation
  — with your work group in terms of fairness and trust, and in being a good communicator and a good listener
- The authority of performance, giving an assurance of quality, of cost-effectiveness and of target achievement
- An ability to use the positive aspects of your organisation culture, and a facility to 'make your boss look good'.

How much power you have and how you use it is in your hands.

When you are on top of your job take on the hard assignments — that's where reputations are made.

Much of this chapter has described the traditional dimensions of the supervisory role but today there are wider demands and new imperatives each with its own priorities.

The following mind map identifies many of these. Look at them in the context of your own organisation and amend it as appropriate. You can expect to meet these pressures and you will be required to set optimum priorities. Your time management must be good.

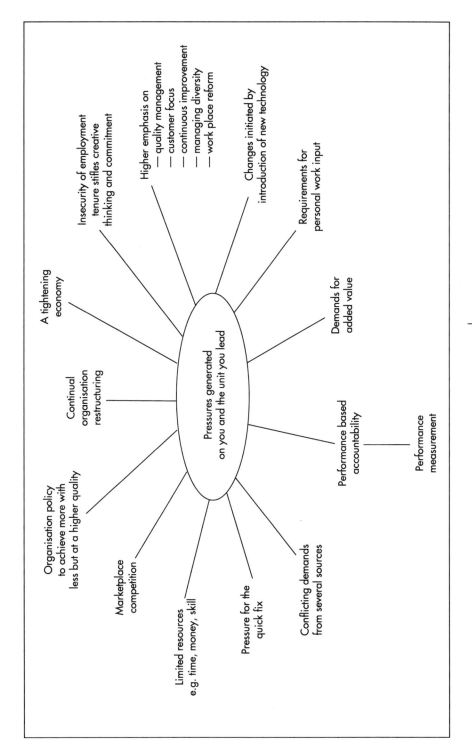

# CHAPTER 3

# MANAGING YOUR TIME

Diagnosing Time Problems
Establishing Priorities
Dealing with Specific Situations

When you read the requirements of a supervisory position today you probably wondered how on earth all these things could be done in the course of a normal working week. Yet it is clear that somehow they must be fitted in.

It would seem that you have three options

* To work harder
* To work longer
* To work smarter.

And of these the logical choice is to seek to work smarter — to use **Time Management**.

You have all the time there is; there isn't any more. It's not the hours you work that count, it's what you put into those hours. And if you believe that time flies remember that you are the navigator.

The major part of your time should be spent on the many duties of supervision. You will also have some routine work of your own to do, including paper work, but you should try and keep this to under two hours a day. Usually special assignments cannot be anticipated and they may require special efforts of organisation or delegation to fit them in. But each day you should try and make time for some creative work; for planning, for seeking improvements in methods or procedures, and for giving special training or coaching.

## DIAGNOSING TIME PROBLEMS

But if you're going to manage time better you must first identify where you seem to be having trouble now.

For instance, during a typical working week what percentage of your time would you spend with each of these:

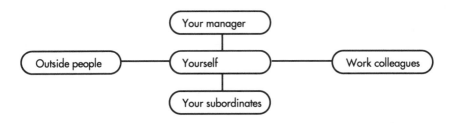

Does this seem about right?

How much of your time is spent on work appropriate to your position, to your level of skill and knowledge?

Where does the rest of it go?

Who interrupts you most?

What can you do about it?

And to further sharpen your diagnosis:

| | A big problem for me | Often a problem | Not a problem |
|---|---|---|---|
| Unclear objectives | | | |
| Changing priorities | | | |
| Inadequate planning | | | |
| No self-imposed deadlines | | | |
| 'Fire-fighting', crises | | | |
| Confused responsibility and authority | | | |
| Personal disorganisation/ cluttered desk | | | |
| Unfinished tasks | | | |
| Duplication of effort | | | |
| Lack of decision | | | |
| Meetings | | | |
| Mixed messages | | | |
| Communication breakdown | | | |
| Incomplete information | | | |

23

| | A big problem for me | Often a problem | Not a problem |
|---|---|---|---|
| Dependence upon grapevine | | | |
| Procrastination | | | |
| Ineffective delegation | | | |
| Change badly handled | | | |
| Inability to say 'no' | | | |
| Ineffective control information | | | |
| Telephone interruptions | | | |
| Unplanned visitors | | | |
| Excessive reports/returns | | | |
| Untrained subordinates | | | |
| Work flow bottlenecks | | | |

Do you include 'discretionary time' in your planning — time for creative thinking, reviewing, developing? This, too, is a necessary part of your job.

Now looking back at your problem items

What can you change? Now?

What will you need help to change?

What must you accept as it is? Why?

You should set specific targets for action, and regularly review progress.

> Time management has three components; the need to
>
> - Establish priorities
> - Use realistic scheduling or programming
> - Learn to make basic decisions and to act on them

Your strength will lie in your ability to manage your priorities. One of the most effective ways of doing this is to classify every task you have to do into one of three groups

Category A — top priority, needing your personal action

Category B — important but not top priority

Category C — can be left until all As and Bs are dealt with.

Then you do your most important A job first and you work through in this sequence not touching a B or a C job (unless its category has changed) while any A is incomplete.

A daily control sheet can be useful.

This can be maintained either on printed sheets or in a pocket notebook.

| Action today | | | Date: | | |
|---|---|---|---|---|---|
| **Priority** | **Job** | | | **A** | **B** | **C** |
| | | | | | | |

But the major problem of most supervisors here is **a failure to focus**, to stay with the priority job instead of being side-tracked into a range of other tasks which need attention.

Seek for techniques which will assist you to overcome your time problems. For instance

- Be aware that some 20 per cent of your effort will usually produce 80 per cent of your results, and identify that 20 per cent (this is important)
- With your manager, challenge every report and return you are required to produce to see if it can be eliminated or simplified
- Try to avoid going to meetings which do not have
    stated start and finish times
    a clear objective
    an agenda
- Control your visitors. Say, for example, 'It's good to see you but I am somewhat busy — will ten minutes be OK?' then after ten minutes you stand up and ease them out (if it's appropriate)
- Identify your priorities and do not procrastinate
- Can you say 'No'?
- If your job takes you away from base stay away until that particular task is finished — notes made, report written
- Use a dictaphone for your own quick recall of contacts and meetings
- If you have a cluttered desk, there are only four options for dealing with paper
    act on it
    refer it to someone else
    file it for reference
    dump it
- Ask yourself 'Am I running my job or is my job running me? Am I really indispensable?'
- What more could you delegate? Why don't you?
- What happens if you are ill or you take leave?

In a time of crisis — and there are plenty of these — don't panic.
　　Pause and ask yourself three questions
　　　　What's actually going on here?
　　　　What's my objective?
　　　　What options do I have?
Then decide what to do.

**Meetings** — sometimes defined as gatherings where they keep the minutes and waste the hours — can be major time consumers. If you have to lead meetings learn the techniques of chairing so that the procedures are
　　formal but friendly
　　fair to all
　　focused on objectives
　　fast but not rushed
　　finished on time with agreed resolution.

If you attend but do not chair and procedures are slow ask for a summary of progress or suggest possible courses of action.

26

If you are required to contribute to only one agenda item seek to attend just for that item.

In the minutes of meetings each item should nominate the person responsible for on-going action.

On the wall of every meeting room the following notice should be clearly displayed:

> Every meeting should have clear answers to
>
> Why are we meeting at all?
> 　　to communicate information?
> 　　to solve problems?
> 　　to make decisions?
> 　　or ......................?
>
> What should we have achieved by the end of the meeting?

The effective supervisor has a realistic concern for the proper use of time for the quality of working life depends upon this. Skill shown here will be reflected in many other areas — people who cannot manage time can seldom manage anything else.

You have active tasks which work towards the achievement of objectives and reactive tasks which deal with the events and crises of the day
　　do you keep them in balance?
　　do you take time out to reassess your priorities?

You have other key responsibilities and a need for enrichment away from the work place:

family

social and community interests

your own development.

If you should collapse on the job from overwork who do you think is really going to worry?

**It's your time — it's your life.**

# PART 2

## THE CORE SKILLS

# CHAPTER 4

# SETTING OBJECTIVES AND PLANNING THE WORK

## YOUR VISION

Before any activity can commence or an organisation be established someone must have a vision of 'what could be' — an ideal to aim for. Then it becomes a matter of expressing this vision in such a way that people will follow it because they want to. This is the mark of a leader — to transfer a vision to people who see its purpose and who accept ownership of it and a commitment to its achievement.

Do you have a vision of what your unit could do and could be? This will give the motivating power to your leadership.

## YOUR MISSION STATEMENT

Every organisation must have a policy. This is a statement of intent or of purpose which sets out clearly why it is in business. For instance, the policy of an airline might be 'the carriage of passengers and freight by air on time, safely, at a profit'. All of its activities should be geared to this and it should be known and understood by every person who works there.

This mission statement is needed

- To establish a consistent, comprehensive and clear purpose to which the whole organisation can relate
- To provide a reference point for strategic planning decisions
- To gain continuing commitment from all staff
- To gain understanding and support from those outside the organisation.

> What is the mission statement of your organisation?
> Does everyone in your unit know it?
> Should they? Why?

But it is quite likely that this gives an overview of the whole enterprise and as such it may not be particularly relevant to what your unit does and therefore your people don't feel overly enthusiastic about it.

What is your unit's unique contribution to the organisation's activities?

Why not discuss this with your people and prepare your own **Unit Mission Statement** which can be displayed with pride?

The Mission Statement is the first stage in the business or organisational plan.

## YOUR ORGANISATIONAL PLAN

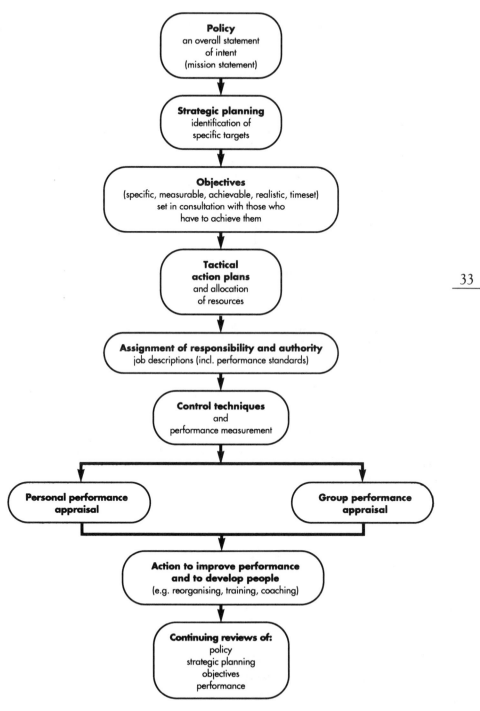

33

## STRATEGIC PLANNING

This is where management decide what must be done if the mission of the organisation is to be achieved.
Strategic planning is a function of senior management.
Typical questions which a company might address would be

- Who are our competitors and what are our and their strengths and weaknesses?
- What are the current trends in our markets? How are these likely to change? What do we see as opportunities and threats?
- What factors (social, economic, political, technological or competitive) are likely to influence our activities over the next three years?
- If present trends continue how do we see this organisation in three years' time?
- How firm is our financial base?
- Will we have the right people in place? Fully competent?
- How will we track changes in the environment in which we operate? Do we have an adequate management information system?

From these considerations would emerge clear targets and priorities for action.

As a supervisor you would probably not get involved in these discussions but you have activities and contacts in quite different fields from those of senior management and often a different information base. Therefore, it is quite possible that you might acquire knowledge of trends or data which could be most useful in this planning and which you should pass on through your manager.

> The essence of management, and of supervision, is to have clear:
>
> **Objectives**
> **Plans**
> **Action**
> **Control**
>
> for these delineate the reasons for your employment.
> Other factors are important. These are critical.

## SETTING OBJECTIVES

Following strategic planning the objectives must be set. An objective means a commitment to projected outcomes of activity and is expressed as an expected result. As such it should be

specific
measurable
achievable
realistic
timeset.

Without this definition it will be an imprecise hope and the subsequent evaluation of effectiveness will be equally vague. Moreover, without such a target people can become very busy, even excessively so, on peripheral activities which may have minimal relationship to bottom line results.

A simple objective statement might read. 'I will ... to achieve ... by ...', and a test of its validity is to ask 'from what, to what, by when?'

Objectives do not exist by themselves, they exist in a time span. Then if they are to be translated into action plans and followed through to achievement these **objectives should be so communicated that they generate a shared sense of purpose and direction throughout the organisation**.

Unless each member of your group knows at all times what the objectives are and what progress is being made towards their achievement why should they care about performance targets? It's just a job.

35

**Feedback on results is a key motivator.**

> How do you formulate objectives so that your work group takes ownership of them and becomes committed to their achievement? Be specific.

One of your tasks is to create a team of above average people who want to do above average work.

— This is a measure of your effectiveness as a supervisor.

But because today things change so very quickly **every objective and every plan should be systematically reviewed every 90 days.**

You and your manager should diary these reviews.

Some organisations have now adopted the practice of **Performance Management** which has given a new emphasis to the setting of objectives. Performance management is a system of

- Job evaluation to establish base or benchmark remuneration levels for defined positions
- Preparing the job description

---

### Setting an Objective

Unit:


**I will accept that we have succeeded if we have:** .............................
(name the objective, quantified if possible)




**Under these conditions:** ....................................................
(state the conditions, restrictions, '*given that*')




**An acceptable outcome will have these characteristics:** ................
(standards of quality and other criteria by which success will be judged)




**And it will be completed by:** ...........................................
(date)


**With progress reviews on:** .............................................
(date/s)

---

- The definition of individual accountability through agreed specific objectives covering the financial year — subject to regular reviews during that year and modification where necessary
- Appraisal of actual performance geared to these objectives which will then be reflected in salary recognition.

The principle is based on results rather than on other criteria.

Criticism of performance management suggests it reinforces the quick fix and that it is difficult to relate it to longer term projects or to staff positions. It can also be upset by the rapidity and complexity of changing situations.

## PLANNING

Planning means looking into the future and preparing for it — it is the thinking that precedes the doing of a piece of work. It is a deliberate effort to answer five questions

- What is the job we are going to do?
- What results are expected? By when?
- What resources are needed?
- Who will do it?
- What is the best way to do it?

It must involve the future, people and action, and it should combine facts and imagination. Without this it could be strong in assertion and weak in reasoning.

People expect to work to a set plan prepared by the person in charge and to be controlled according to that plan, but they know that adjustments may be needed to meet changing circumstances.

If planning is well done the rest of the task becomes easier. It is not something done just once. Conditions may change at any time, and plans must be reviewed constantly, perhaps weekly or daily or even hourly. A good supervisor does a blend of brain work and active work, and time must be allowed for your planning.

How you plan in your particular job will depend on what has to be done. Here are three different approaches — you should develop the one which is most appropriate

### A

- Identify your purpose — clearly
- State specific objectives
- Assign responsibility, authority and accountability
- Nominate measurable activities

37

- Establish control procedures
- Evaluate results.

**B**

- Identify the target
- Set a unit of performance measurement
- Set the required output standard
- Identify the indicators of deviation
- Instal an appropriate control function.

**C**

### 1 Objectives

Do you know quite clearly what has to be done and by when? What standard of performance or production is needed? What are the critical factors?

### 2 Resources

(a) People — do you know the abilities of each person in your group? Will they all be available during the period you are planning for?

(b) Equipment and materials — will everything be there when it is needed? If necessary, can you get replacements or additional stock? Is maintenance or servicing available?

(c) Authority — do you need any special approvals?

(d) Is timing adequate?

(e) Is finance available and authorised?

### 3 Work flow

Do you know where your work comes from and where it goes to? How dependent are you on the work of other units? Can the work be planned so that everyone is kept fully occupied on work that suits their skills, and so that there are no bottlenecks or crises?

### 4 Controls

What controls will be necessary on this work — time, cost, quality, quantity, other. Where will close supervision be necessary? How will these controls be set up and maintained?

### 5 Contingency planning

The timing of some tasks is fixed, while for others it may be varied. If necessary, which can be postponed and for how long? Which demands priority? If you were absent what would happen? Have understudies been trained for key tasks?

In some cases a written contingency plan can be useful, for instance:

| What could go wrong or change the plan? | Is this likely or significant? | Preventive action — what can I do to keep this from happening? | Contingency action— what will I do if it happens anyway? |
|---|---|---|---|
| | | | |
| | | | |
| | | | |
| | | | |
| | | | |
| | | | |
| | | | |

One component of planning which is sometimes necessary is the use of **standard time**.

This is the time estimated to do a specific work output. It is calculated as the time it would take an average employee working at an average pace to do a task of defined quantity and quality, plus an allowance for work interruptions, fatigue and personal time. When used it will have been discussed with and agreed to by the union. When work measurement is possible this becomes a device for determining staffing requirements.

For small or for routine tasks your planning may be quite straight-forward and follow a set pattern, but for a special project or a large job you may find it helpful to prepare a written plan. This should set out each step in order and show the following:

| (a)<br>What must<br>be done<br>and by<br>when | (b)<br>Who will<br>do it | (c)<br>Plant, equipment<br>or material<br>needed | (d)<br>Action needed<br>to make sure<br>that (b) and<br>(c) are ready | (e)<br>Priority |
|---|---|---|---|---|
|  |  |  |  |  |

It is important to number in a priority order the jobs to be done, but you should review this often for priorities can and do change. Do you need to plan for alternative courses of action?

For some supervisors a desk calendar can be an effective planning aid:

| | **Tuesday** | **10 November** |
|---|---|---|
| 8.00 | Check absences — rearrange jobs | |
| 8.30 | | |
| 9.00 | Peter — cost estimates for Project K | |
| 9.30 | Prepare for budget meeting 9 am Friday | |
| 10.00 | | |
| 10.30 | Coaching Jim on new stat control | |
| 11.00 | | |
| 11.30 | Mgr re info for annual report | |

You must plan the work of your unit, but you cannot do it in isolation. Also you must know what other people are doing and how their work may affect your plan. You should discuss this with your manager to find out how it will fit in with other activities it is associated with or may be part of. How important is timing? Will other units want to use plant or equipment at the same time as you? What possible difficulties can be expected? Are there special conditions you should know about?

You should also know what other supervisors whose work is related to yours are planning to do, and they should be told of your work plan.

The people in your unit will take it for granted that you do plan every job and they have a right to expect that the work will go smoothly without crisis, wastage, accident or confusion.

Take time to plan. It will save many hours and many dollars. A typical job may look like this:

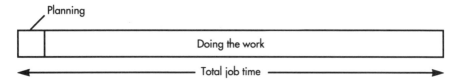

But research has shown that if you spend three times as long planning, the total job time can usually be reduced by some 33.3 per cent.

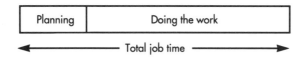

41

Don't be stampeded into action until you have thought through the possible results of what you will do. **Don't let the pressure of immediate problems make you lose sight of your real objective**. This is always a danger. Someone has said that when you are up to your knees in alligators it is difficult to remember that your main objective is to drain the swamp.

Make your own luck. Luck occurs when planning meets opportunity.

Plans will fail if there is
    lack of understanding of the problem or the objective
    insufficient time for planning, leading to expediency action
    inadequate consideration of the alternatives
    failure to supply sufficient information to those involved
    misunderstanding, misjudgement, bad timing
    defect in the control system.

One objective in much of the planning you have to do should be to increase **productivity** — this is more than production, it is the return on the investment in the organisation, the ratio between the input resources of people, equipment, etc., and the output they produce. This can refer to
    output per labour hour
    output per unit of material or equipment
    output per unit of capital or to
    other elements.

It is just as important in government and local body activities as it is in the private sector.

The more efficient organisations devote considerable attention to ensure the continuing optimum utilisation of these measures and monitor them regularly.

## ORGANISING

This is a process of translating your plans into action. It means that

— for each task a person has to do there should be one clear and defined source of authority (this is known as unity of command). If two people are giving instructions in the same area of activity confusion and conflict are inevitable

— no supervisor should be made responsible for more people than he or she can effectively control (called span of control)

— tasks should be grouped into 'one person parcels' of related jobs

— responsibility should be delegated to the lowest effective level .at which all the facts are known

— supervisors should not be bypassed when instructions or information are passed to employees

— criticism of an employee should be done privately

— a person whose work is subject to regular inspection should be given the assistance and facilities necessary for maintaining an independent check of performance quality.

These are some of the basic rules for good team work. But organising requires the use of other resources. It means, for instance, that

finance is available and cash flow is maintained

adequate controls are in place

continuous feedback is maintained

work is fairly allocated

people have been properly trained and coached

there is good communication

materials, tools, equipment are ready and available when needed

there are no safety hazards

the work flow is not impeded

waste is held to a minimum

time is properly used,

and generally that all resources are so used that work objectives are constantly met and that high morale is maintained.

42

## FINANCIAL MANAGEMENT

It will cost money to run your unit — wages or salaries, materials or equipment, operating costs, a percentage of overheads, etc. It is a cost centre. You may or may not be revenue earning. Therefore, it is essential that you find out from your manager or your accountant the financial expectations from your unit.

- The budgeted costs of operating the unit: direct and indirect
- The budgeted income.

Budgeted figures set limits, but today the overriding aim is to achieve better results with less input. This can be done only by the sustained efforts of the whole unit, so financial targets and their attainment should be a regular topic for discussion at staff meetings with cost benefit analysis constantly in mind.

If you are in a commercial enterprise it is important to get your priorities right. The primary task is to generate sufficient cash flow to ensure the continuation of the business. Only then do you deal with trading problems of sales and profit. Many business failures can be attributed to overlooking this. If it is appropriate to do so you should constantly use your accountant as an on-going financial adviser rather than a remote keeper of the books, and you must understand the meanings of the accounting terms in general use.

43

## Budgets

You will be expected to operate within approved budgets. A budget is a planned allocation of the resources available, broken down into 'programmes' for each area of activity, showing the amount allowed for the period or the year. It is usually expressed in money terms, but it may refer to materials or to people. This sets an upper limit within which you are expected to operate and to meet your objectives.

It will probably be broken down into weekly or four-weekly figures and the control system will enable you to compare performance with budget for each period.

Your group should be aware of their budget and performance.

But the budget is set to a predetermined limit and your adherence to it is only one measure of effectiveness. Another criterion is what you actually accomplished within this constraint — what you did with what you had. You should constantly be asking, with hindsight, what more could you have done?

## Managing Costs

Survival in the commercial world is dependent upon maintaining adequate profit. Profit — the surplus from trading — is sales revenue less total costs, but from this profit non-trading payments must be made for taxation, loan repayments, shareholders' returns and provision for growth. The pressure points are sales and costs, and the continuing target for supervisors is the need to reduce costs. This is discussed further in Chapter 5 under Performance Measurement but one must be aware of the presence of hidden costs particularly those incurred by under-utilised resources, physical and human.

What under-utilised resources can you identify in your work unit?

## Stock Management

If your unit uses plant, equipment, or materials your financial responsibility increases for you will be ordering and holding stock for which there will be costs of space, heating, fittings, lighting, maintenance and obsolescence. You should identify the minimum stock you must carry to meet immediate operational needs and ensure that your suppliers hold stock which will be available on call just in time to maintain the requirements of your work flow. This 'Just In Time' (JIT) policy is the key to effective stock management but it demands high standards of coordination and communication between users and providers and must be subject to continuous review. Performance accountability must be clearly assigned.

# MARKETING

Marketing is the combination of skills, decisions and activities required in identifying, anticipating and satisfying (and perhaps exceeding) the customer's needs and desires. It is part of the planning process — and it applies to all positions.

The mechanism of selling is persuasion.

In your job you may not be directly involved with customers outside the organisation but you will have in-house customers. Every task has a

- Provider — where the work comes from
- The point of action
- Customer — where the product or service passes to.

Each has expectations of the other and the three parties should meet informally but regularly to discuss how the work flow might be handled more effectively and where improvement could be initiated.

Most tasks move cross-functionally and such meetings play a significant part in improving co-operation and coordination between units. This eliminates the danger of unit teams becoming too inward-looking or competitive. The competition should be outside the organisation.

If you do have outside customers remember that nothing is accomplished until the sale is completed and the money is in the bank. This means that every member of your unit must be competent in the techniques associated with selling and maintaining customer relationships.

Any organisation which does not meet fully the expectations of its customers or clients will fail.

**Your job, no matter what it may be, exists only to meet the needs of your customers whether they be in-house or external.**

And every member of your unit needs to be very aware of this.

This has wider implications if the work of your unit passes a product or service to external customers for here

- Your unit is seen by the customer to represent the whole organisation
- You have hands-on responsibility for not only the quality and the presentation or delivery of the product or service, but also for the behavioural impact of the people in your unit.
  — the unthinking action of one of your people could lose your organisation a major client, and you would carry much of the blame.

45

The CARE philosophy should underpin all the things your unit does — Customers Are Really Everything.

Don't overlook marketing — your customers are the people for whom you provide goods, services or information and their assessment of this will be based upon how well you meet their continuing expectations.

You should constantly identify (a) who are your customers/clients — can you group them into categories? and (b) what are their particular needs? Then when you have ascertained these needs you should ask how fully your unit/group or organisation meets all of these needs and what you should be doing to fill the gaps. That is marketing.

Your customers don't deal with organisations — they deal with people. Who are the individuals who are the nearest to your customers? How well trained are they? What customer feedback do you get? Switchboard operators, receptionists and people who write letters are your most important public relations contacts.

**Customer/Client:**

| Services need: | Product need: |
|---|---|
| We offer: | |

Performance, image and service are the demonstration of voluntary commitment.

Every job in your organisation carries a marketing responsibility.

# CHAPTER 5

# GETTING THE WORK DONE

## ALLOCATING WORK

Most supervisors are competent in doing the work they now supervise, but they may find it difficult to allocate work to others.

You are not being paid to do the work yourself — you were appointed to get work done by other people so you must give them productive work to do. There are two stages in this

- First you must know how capable each person is
- Then you must assign work to them.

One way to handle the first step is to prepare a **Capability Chart** for your unit, and to keep it up to date by a regular review. It should show:

| Reviewed on // //:// | | Each job the unit has to do | | | | | | Notes |
|---|---|---|---|---|---|---|---|---|
| | | **1** | **2** | **3** | **4** | **5** | **6** | |
| | A | Δ | | | Δ̄ | | Δ | |
| Names of people in | B | / | Δ | Δ | Δ | | Δ̄ | |
| the unit | C | | | | | Δ | Δ | |
| | D | | ∧ | Δ | Δ | | ∧ | |
| | E | Δ | Δ | / | / | | | Train (3) by 1 June |
| | F | ∧ | | Δ̄ | Δ | | / | |

/ = is being trained on this job
∧ = partly trained but still needs supervision — or, can do the job but has not yet acquired speed
Δ = fully competent on this job both for quality and for speed
Δ̄ = competent to teach this job to others.

48

From such a review, which should be compiled in discussion with your staff, several things may be learned. For instance, in this example
— B may be ready either for promotion or for transfer to gain further experience in another unit
— A should be given training in one of the other jobs
— job 5 should be examined immediately. What will happen if C is away, and why has no one else been trained on it? If the supervisor has to do it, who then runs the unit?
— you should plan to have an understudy available for each position. **Multi-skilling is now an objective in most organisations.**
— what other training should be started? What target dates should be set for this?

You will probably find that your people will respond to the challenge of this review. It generates pride and a desire to attain competency in all the tasks. It will give more purpose to skill learning.

The review can tell you what 'people resource' you have. You may also need to know what 'equipment resource' you have, particularly if you have to share it (perhaps a vehicle) with other units.
When allocating work to people you should ensure that

• Work output requirements are clearly defined
• Each person will be fully and productively occupied
• Back up and support is available if needed.

A Work Plan can be useful, for instance:

| People in the unit1 | September (Working days) | | | | | | | | | | | | | | | | | | | | | | |
|---|---|---|---|---|---|---|---|---|---|---|---|---|---|---|---|---|---|---|---|---|---|---|---|
| | 1 | 2 | 3 | 6 | 7 | 8 | 9 | 10 | 13 | 14 | 15 | 16 | 17 | 20 | 21 | 22 | 23 | 24 | 27 | 28 | 29 | 30 |
| A | | | | | | | | | | | | | | | | | | | | | | |
| B | | | | | | | | | | | | | | | | | | | | | | |
| C | | | | | | | | | | | | | | | | | | | | | | |
| D | | | | | | | | | | | | | | | | | | | | | | |
| E | | | | | | | | | | | | | | | | | | | | | | |
| F | | | | | | | | | | | | | | | | | | | | | | |

Jobs can be given a number or a simple coding.

Suitable marks can be added to show the various stages of completion
of these jobs or other relevant data such as who has the prime responsibility for action.

Keep a stock of blank Work Planning Charts for use at any time. Until you are used to it, give yourself plenty of time both to prepare a chart and to check it. Checking ensures that nothing has been overlooked. You will find this a most valuable tool.

## THE WORK FLOW

Work flow concerns the passage of work through your unit. It is your job to ensure that this goes through smoothly all the time, and that there

— are no slack periods when people are waiting for work
— is enough time for checking, testing, or inspection
— is a correct sequence of operations so that there is no bottleneck or duplication of effort
— are no unnecessary movements by people or materials
— is a continuing review of work methods to see whether there may be a better way of achieving the objective
— is provision for training and coaching.

You should examine

1  The layout of the work place:
   (a)  does it give a steady and uninterrupted work flow or can it be improved? Do people have to move around too much to do their work?

    (b)  is the housekeeping as good as it should be — clean, free from obstructions or untidiness, with adequate storage or stowage?

    (c)  are there any safety hazards?

2  The work station of each person:

    (a)  is it adequate for the work that has to be done?

    (b)  does it cause unnecessary fatigue?

    (c)  are all materials required readily available?

    (d)  are light, heating and ventilation adequate?

3  Equipment and machines:

    (a)  can they do the job?

    (b)  are they being used properly? fully?

    (c)  are they properly serviced or maintained?

    (d)  are all safety requirements being observed?

> Are you living with known defects or deficiencies? Why?

    Work flow affects everyone in the unit. You should discuss it with them and seek and be receptive to their ideas and their suggestions for improvement.

## MANAGING YOUR RESOURCES

You have many resources — more, perhaps, than you realise. Each must be identified, then examined regularly to ensure that you are getting the optimum value from them.

Consider, for instance

(a)  Financial management

    — what are the financial expectations from the work of your unit? e.g. costs — direct and indirect, income generated, debt incurred

    — do activities affect cash flow?

    — are all activities cost-effective?

    — what more could be achieved within budget?

    — are all staff aware of bottom line imperatives and cost conscious in task performance?

(b)  Information technology

    — does your unit receive all the information it needs (and not more) in a form you can use and when you need it?

(c)  Inventory

    — are you carrying too much or too little?

    — have JIT principles been introduced?

(d)  Advisory services
    — various people supply information or services to your unit —
      accountants, stores, administration, computer people, personnel
      department, etc., many of whom want reports or data from you.
      How often do you initiate a discussion with them to explore how
      these points of contact might be made more effective?
    — can you make better use of their expertise? For instance, a manage-
      ment accountant (compared with someone who just keeps the
      books) should be assisting your organisation in assessing risks,
      analysing money markets, developing a money sense throughout
      the organisation, pointing sales people into profitable directions,
      talking with people who spend the money, advising managers and
      supervisors on real budgeting, checking capital investments for
      optimum returns, etc.

Other elements of this are raised in the section on 'Continuous
Improvement', but the key point here is that profitable outcomes are
dependent wholly upon your own initiative.

51

## PERFORMANCE MEASUREMENT

In every field of endeavour knowledge of results is essential for understanding, for motivation and for progress. Each person at work needs
continuing feedback on
    'Tell me what you expect of me.'
    'Tell me how am I performing. What's the score?'
Teams are particularly vocal in demanding this information.
    Performance management is the process designed to meet this need,
but another question has been added, 'compared with what?', which requires
(a) a target or a yardstick against which performance may be measured,
and (b) people able to take appropriate remedial action. Much will depend
upon the precision with which objectives have been set. For instance,
measurement is almost impossible if an objective states 'Our aim is to
raise our standards of supervision.' From what? To what? By when?
    You are employed to get work done, so you will need some controls to
make certain that it is being done and done properly.
    Control means supplying to you or to those in key positions the infor-
mation necessary to know whether the objectives are being achieved, in
all respects.
Each control you use should have three elements
    to set standards (quantity, quality, cost, time, etc)
    to measure performance
    to correct deviations from the standard.

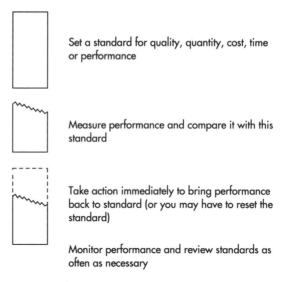

Set a standard for quality, quantity, cost, time or performance

Measure performance and compare it with this standard

Take action immediately to bring performance back to standard (or you may have to reset the standard)

Monitor performance and review standards as often as necessary

> The technique of
> — setting a standard
> — measuring what is actually happening
> — taking corrective action either by modifying performance or by amending the standard
> — then again measuring performance and taking corrective action
>
> is known as the **control cycle** and is established practice on most production work

An overall aim is to improve productivity

$$\text{Productivity} = \frac{\text{total output}}{\text{total input}} = \frac{\text{total results achieved}}{\text{total resources consumed}}$$

For instance, if 12 units of output were produced using 6 units of labour productivity would be 2.

In the rating of performance the 'significant few' factor (the Pareto distribution) is important. This has demonstrated across a wide spectrum of activities that 20 per cent of effort generates 80 per cent of the results, and vice versa. So one should therefore concentrate effort on the 20 per cent elements. Activities within this area are usually called **Key Performance Indicators,** but the term KPI refers also to specific tasks for which accountability has been assigned.

Management, of course, must identify which key activities shall be subject to regular performance measurement review. The range of choice is wide, for instance:

(a)  Broadly they could relate to
      Stock
      Production
      Sales
      Finance and Budget
      Personnel
      Customers
      and

(b)  More specifically to
      Equipment/Tools: output per hour
                   percentage of capacity used
                   percentage of cost over total cost
                   percentage of down time
                   output per person hour
                   percentage of labour cost over total cost
                   percentage of productive time over total time

      Capital: ratio of operating profit to operating assets
              net profit margin
              asset turnover

      Sales: calls per person per day
             average return per call
             average cost per call
             new and lost customers per period
                     etc.

A form of recording performance measurement data is illustrated below.

One heading needs explanation: 'benchmarking' in this context means an analysed comparison with identical or similar activities elsewhere
— within the organisation
— within the industry (nationally or internationally)
— compared with recorded trends.

These reports should be made available promptly to the unit concerned and be the subject of a staff meeting to discuss points arising and to plan on-going action.

To be effective performance measurement reports must be

• Related to the work and not to those who do it
• The frequency should be determined by the situation
• Measurement should relate to objectives (graphs and charts may be more realistic than figures)

54

Performance Measurement Report

| Activity: | Period: |
|---|---|
| Source of data: | Target: |
| Report for this period: | |
| Special features: | |
| Comparison with previous periods: | |
| Benchmark comparisons: | |
| Action now arising: | |

- The compilation, the feedback and the action planning should be with those who carried out the activity. If there are defects there should also be praise. The aim is improvement.

Now, to look more specifically at your performance controls:
Consider each control operating in your areas of activity

- Does each do exactly what it should?
- Is it a fast operational control or a historical report to senior staff?
- What recent breakdowns in control have occurred? Were they due to undercontrolling, to overcontrolling?
- What necessary information don't you get?

How is accountability monitored where you work?

**Failure to define and assign accountability — and to make it stick — is a major weakness in many organisations today.**
Your skill in operating effective controls is a key measure of your own competency, and is probably the most difficult to maintain.

It is essential that you remember at all times that:

55

> **Whatever you accept you approve**

Your people know only one standard — what you accept is good work.
This means that if one of your people is doing work that is not wholly up to the standard required and you do nothing about it then you are openly saying to that person and to others in the group 'you have my full permission to do poor work'. And you're in deep trouble.
All jobs must meet an agreed and accepted standard (a 'pass mark') and if you are developing your group as a team there must be continuous

- Accountability
  individuals being clear on and committed to what they are expected to do
- Feedback
  telling people what is happening and what is going to happen and reporting factually on performance matched with targets
- Recognition
  of individual and group performance
- Training and coaching
  for improvement and growth.

Your primary concern must be the commitment of the group to the objectives. And you are dealing with the group as a whole, at the same time being aware of the contribution of each individual, for

> Peer pressure is the strongest motivator

As your group becomes a team taking pride in high standard work they will assume a team responsibility for goal achievement and your 'control' role will become more as a monitor of performance, leading rather than telling.

There are several forms of control which are used. But you should use only those which are necessary, because over-controlling causes resentment and is as bad a fault as under-controlling.

You should discuss with your manager which controls you should use, and whether or not they should be modified.

56

## Cost Control

Purpose: to ensure that those costs within the supervisor's power to control are, in fact, being controlled.
The elements of costs are those related to

- Direct labour
    the wages of those concerned with the making of the product or with performance
- Indirect labour
    the wages of those in service departments such as stores, maintenance, personnel and administration
- Direct materials
    raw materials allocated to the product, components or sub-assemblies
- Indirect materials
    all consumables, such as oil, grease, cleaning materials, and small items, such as nuts and bolts
- Direct expenses
    all expenses other than labour or materials which are charged directly to the job; for example, plans and specifications
- Indirect expenses
    running expenses, such as electricity, gas, water, rates, rent and insurance.

These are sometimes shown in another way:

| Direct materials | Direct labour | Factory expense | Administration expense | Selling expense |
|---|---|---|---|---|
| Prime cost | | | | |
| Factory cost | | | | |
| Manufacturing cost | | | | |
| Total cost | | | | |

You may also need to know three types of costing systems

- Job costing
  this is where the job is 'one off' or 'custom built' and all costs are charged directly to the job
- Standard costing
  where costs are estimated in advance, or predetermined, and the actual costs can then be compared with this standard
- Process costing
  where the job is costed stage by stage until it is completed.

It is important that you know which costs occur in those areas which come within your field of work for you can influence these. You will need this information regularly from your manager so that you can detect any variations, and note where they happen. Then, if you can take corrective action you should do so.

It is quite likely that you will be told to try to reduce costs. If this happens you will need to look closely at each item, giving special attention to the need to

- Reduce waste
  waste can occur with wrongly used raw materials, with scrap, breakages, poor maintenance, or by people being incorrectly or underemployed.
- Save time
  can output be increased, machines or equipment be better used, or work flow be improved?
- Use space more intelligently
  space for storage, for production or for freight costs a lot of money. Can it be reduced?
- Use people properly
  how long does it take a new employee to become fully productive?
Can this be done better and faster? What can you do to reduce labour turnover or absenteeism? Are the skills that people have being fully and properly used? How effective are your training procedures?

57

- Reduce movement

    what movements do people, materials, paper, etc. have to go through to achieve their purposes?

But note — all your employees will have their own ideas on cutting corners or reducing waste, so don't hesitate to consult them.

If you had a directive to reduce your costs by 6 per cent by the end of next month what would you do?

Why don't you?

> The easiest way to make money is to stop losing it

## Production or Performance Control

Purpose: to keep production or performance up to a nominated level and to set standards.

Production is sometimes shown as a percentage figure:

$$\frac{\text{Actual production}}{\text{Standard production set}} \times \frac{100}{1}$$

Your unit may not get detailed cost statements, but may use figures for person-day or person-hour production or some other defined target as its measure. A suggested method is a simple graph which you can maintain to compare performance and target at regular intervals, for example:

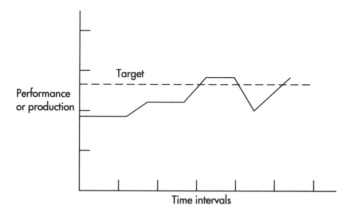

## Deadline Control

Purpose: to ensure (a) that work is being finished on time; or (b) that adequate progress is being made on jobs.

Suggested methods: (a) wall chart listing to show when jobs are due and from whom. The person responsible to initial when completed; and (b) if the job is a long one, prepare a bar graph for the estimated target date and block in parts as completed. Self-maintained.

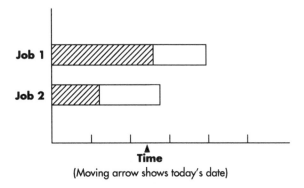

(Moving arrow shows today's date)

## Work Survey Control

Purpose: to ensure that no jobs are overlooked, that jobs have the right priorities, and that everyone is fully occupied.

Suggested method: a weekly review of all unfinished work within the unit, job by job, or person by person. Self-maintained.

## Work Scheduling Control

Purpose: to avoid overloading people and to control work output where repetitive jobs are handled.

Suggested method: estimate or measure the time required for each section of the work, group related jobs into one-person assignments, allocate them to individual members of the unit, and set realistic deadlines for completion. Self-maintained

## Control by Exception

Purpose: to identify the specific problems which require the personal attention of the supervisor or manager.

Suggested method: set a performance standard and a tolerance range and instruct that immediately the output figures fall outside that range you are to be notified.

This gives more responsibility to subordinates and frees the supervisor for other activity. But the validity of the standards should be checked regularly.

## Fault Location Control

Purpose: to pinpoint sources of error in complex repetitive jobs so that corrections may be made and training given.

Suggested method: chart all the stages of the operation and the people employed, then study details of the processes and record precisely where errors occur. **And**, encourage the operators to help in this, for the objective is improvement and greater efficiency at reduced cost, not to blame or to reprimand.

**Fault location chart**

| Job: | Faults detected in each stage of this job (卌 = 5) | | | | | | | |
|---|---|---|---|---|---|---|---|---|
| | I | II | III | IV | V | VI | VII | VIII |
| A | | // | | | 卌 / | / | | |
| B | // | | /// | | /// | | // | |
| C | | | / | / | 卌 /// | | // | |
| D | // | | | / | 卌 | // | | |
| E | | | | | 卌 // | | / | / |
| F | | / | | / | /// | | | / |

(left label: People doing this job — rows A–F)

In this example each of the stages 1–VIII would be clearly identified and described. The key area of concern is clearly stage V where most of the errors are occurring, and this is where correction and retraining is needed.

## Staff Meetings

Purpose: to ensure that all members of the unit understand the objective and what has to be done, and are told how the work is progressing, the difficulties expected, the deadlines to be met, etc.

Suggested method: a regular meeting (perhaps 20 minutes a week) at which views are shared, work is reviewed, and problems discussed.

To be productive these meetings must be planned. For instance:
1  Open the meeting
    start on time
    state the topic and the objectives.
2  Present the topic or problem
    open the discussion
    state the facts, ask a question, give conflicting views. A good starter to get involvement is to ask 'What is going well?' and 'What's getting in the way?'
3  Conduct the discussion
    ask rather than tell
    encourage comment, ideas and exchange of experiences

  ask open-ended questions — what, why, where, how?
  avoid personalities
  separate facts and opinions
  summarise frequently (would a whiteboard help?)
4 Determine action
  review key points
  present conclusions or proposals
  outline action, e.g. who should do what by when.
5 Close the meeting on or before the stated time.

In many organisations the interval between these meetings is now being extended, perhaps to once monthly. It has been found to be most productive to have a five-minute meeting (not longer) at the start of each day to discuss highlights and problems of **yesterday** and expectations of today.

Overall control is most effective when a blend of these or other controls is used, but remember that conditions change sometimes unexpectedly. **No control should be maintained longer than it is clearly seen to be needed. Controls should show pulse beats and record any deviation from the desired pattern so that corrective action can be initiated without delay.**

61

Many controls, including most financial printouts, give historical information which will tell you what happened but not where you are going, and by the time action is taken a lot of loss will have occurred.

> If you can't measure you can't manage

If people know what is being measured, and the reason for it, they will respond.

But there is another side to this which you should know. It is summarised by the statement: What is not inspected will deteriorate.

---

One important facet of performance must be stressed:

**Are you measuring activities or results?**
'Sales booked per day' is activity oriented
'Contribution to sales profit per day' is results oriented

Look over all the control records you are keeping — what are you measuring?

## QUALITY MANAGEMENT

'Quality' has many definitions. To some it is the presence of value and fitness for use as perceived by the customer. To others it is the degree of excellence which satisfies the customers. Some state the aim is to exceed the customers' expectations, while others say it cannot be defined — it is felt emotionally before a definition surfaces. It is cost-effective defect-free action meeting the requirements of customers today and tomorrow.

But two components require clarification

• Quality assurance refers to systems for measuring production against set criteria, using quality tools to a specific end
• Quality improvement is a broader concept incorporating a range of management techniques covering all elements of the operations. It is people focused.

In this context **Total Quality Management** incorporates

QA + Q1 + SPC (Statistical Process Control)

and requires total organisational commitment operationally led by managers and supervisors. The International Standards Association (ISO) has published a series of standards (The ISO 9000 series) through which organisations who meet these standards may gain certification and accreditation which can carry significant recognition in today's highly competitive marketplace. Some purchasers now specify this.

Supervisors have a critical role to play in the continuing quest for quality. The drive must be initiated and maintained from top management downwards — without this the scheme will collapse — but the work force responds to their immediate bosses, the supervisors, and will follow the example they set rather than to the words they use.

*In one company the Managing Director proclaimed 'Here we are fully committed to achieving quality in everything. Our customers expect it and it is now the key factor in all our activities'. Later that afternoon down on the factory floor a supervisor shouted to the work group 'Come on, that order has to go out today — the customer is waiting. Move it! That's good enough, get it out!'*

Quality had already given way to perceived deadlines. Responsibility for quality must be accepted by and be a commitment of every individual at all levels in the organisation. It must be built into all activities it cannot be inspected in. This means that

• New appointees should start work at the quality standards they will be expected to maintain. They will work up to higher quantity output but they will retain the quality set on their first day. This is where you begin building pride in work.

- People should be consulted when quality standards are being set so that they may share in ownership of them. They will then be aware of deviations that can occur and have the ability to take the necessary corrective action.

> Today's quality is tomorrow's reputation

It costs at least six times as much in marketing and advertising to gain a new customer at it does to retain an established customer. To retain customers will require more than just maintaining present standards of service or product — your competitors will constantly be looking for better ways which will give them the market edge. You will be expected to lead your work group in a drive for continuous improvement in everything you do.

> Where you work you set the quality standards — in everything — and this doesn't only mean work. It also means the quality of your communication, your relationships, and your promises. These are observed and you are the role model

63

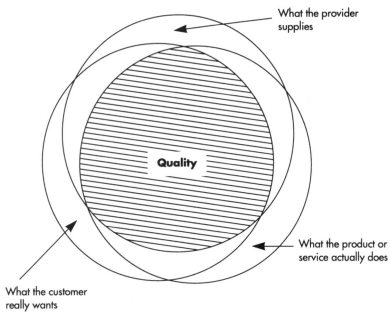

What the provider supplies

Quality

What the product or service actually does

What the customer really wants

**Quality**: your job to provide the best fit

## CONTINUOUS IMPROVEMENT

We live in a constantly competitive environment, and in the work place there is continuous competition for

— market share or public support
— the achievement of profit or effectiveness targets
— customer/client satisfaction
— finance
— resources of all kinds
— recognition of effort
— executive favour.

To stand still is to be knocked over by the following traffic — there are no orderly queues — and every organisation now recognises that there must be continuous improvement in every activity to gain and maintain competitive advantage. This means a need to review systematically and quite ruthlessly everything that your unit does, asking

- What does this activity achieve? (Purpose)
- What is its present status?        (Information)
- Why are we there?                (Analysis)
- Where could/should we be?        (Exploring Options)
- How can we add value?            (Improvement)

- Who should now do what?    (Action Planning)
- Are we getting there?    (Performance measurement and review)

Results should be assessed by productivity gain — costing less to produce or accomplish more or better. A key ingredient in those organisations where productivity continues to increase is that people feel an individual and collective responsibility for solving problems. When something goes wrong or where there is room for improvement they do something about it either by action or by recommendation.

But for these things to happen several conditions must be met

- Your organisation must be committed to quality improvement, and where appropriate to a striving for market leadership in its field
- People at all levels are taught and are competent in problem-solving skills
- Team leadership replaces autocratic control so that people have a sense of ownership in their activities
- Effort is recognised, and there are many ways of doing this.

You should constantly be seeking to improve work methods in your area — to reduce costs, to remove hazards, to do more with less effort, to increase performance, to save time, to cut wastage or spoilage.

Every job can be improved or simplified. There's always a better way. One spur is to keep seeking for more, better, cheaper, faster.

There are three requirements

- A desire and a determination to produce better results
- An understanding of the human factors involved
  - people tend to resist change for it generates feelings of insecurity.
  - they will oppose anything they feel will diminish them. So, if there is to be an effective change it should benefit the people affected.
- An understanding of the economic factors
  costs, savings to be gained, etc.

You and each member of your group should always be on the lookout to ask such questions as

- Could this job be eliminated?
- Could it be combined with some other job?
- Could it be done with less effort or with fewer movements?
- Could it be done in another place or at another time?
- How can we reduce waste of
  money?
  opportunity?
  people's ability?
  unused technology?
  knowledge?

rework or downtime?
inventory?
energy?
space?
transport?

- How can we add value to our product or service?
- Are we living with accepted deficiencies?   (Many people are)

Every function or process, every report or return, should be put on trial for its life at least once a year.

---

If you are not looking for problems how can there be improvement?

---

Creativity has been defined as creative dissatisfaction

The Work Method Examination Sheet which follows is a most useful instrument. If you record carefully what is being done now and compare this with a proposed better way the savings to be made will quickly be apparent to management.

A starter at a staff meeting might be to ask 'What could we do to improve things around here?' Listen, and jointly select a project.

It could be good training for your deputy or one of your team to lead a small task force and to report back to the whole group before a proposal goes forward.

When a new idea or proposal is received look at it carefully and if necessary discuss it with your manager.

---

**To pre-test new ideas**
Answer all questions
1   Will it improve things, e.g. increase productivity, improve quality?
2   Is this a more efficient way to use employees?
3   Will it improve operations, maintenance or construction?
4   Is it an improvement on present methods or equipment?
5   Will it improve safety?
6   Will it reduce waste? Use resources more effectively?
7   Does it reduce/eliminate unnecessary work?
8   Does it lower costs?
9   Will it improve working conditions?
10   Will it differ from existing union arrangements?
11   Will it be supported by the people involved? and finally:
So, what will you do now?

| | What is achieved? | Is it necessary? Why? | What else could be done? | What should be done? |
|---|---|---|---|---|
| **Purpose** | What is achieved? | Is it necessary? Why? | What else could be done? | What should be done? |
| **Place** | Where is it done? | Why there? Advantages? Disadvantages? | Where else could it be done? Advantages? Disadvantages? | Where should it? |
| **Sequence** | Where is it done? After? Before? | Why then? Advantages? Disadvantages? | When else could it be done? Advantages? Disadvantages? | When should it? |
| **Person** | Who does it? | Why that person? Advantages? Disadvantages? | Who else could do it? Advantages? Disadvantages? | Who should? |
| **Method** | How is it done? | Why that way? Advantages? Disadvantages? | How else could it be? Advantages? Disadvantages? | How should it? |
| | I recommend | | | |

**Work method examination sheet — task:**

When you recommend improvements in work methods you should

- State why your proposal has value — what it will do
- Outline the proposal

- Show clearly the advantages to be gained (including savings in costs, time, energy or material, etc.)
- Outline an action plan to show how the proposal can be implemented.

Encourage everyone to make suggestions:

What is a
SUGGESTION?
A constructive idea that
answers YES to any of
the following questions:-

**1** Will it Simplify?
- operations
- methods
- work flow

**2** Will it eliminate?
- waste
- accident hazards
- non-essential routines

**3** Will it improve?
- service to customers
- working conditions
- productivity

**4** Will it establish a new practice?
- that is better
- that is safer
- that is more cost-effective

**5** Will it provide a solution?
- that is understandable
- that is practicable
- that is timely

68

## LOOK WIDELY

In the quest for continuous improvement do not be limited within the range of your daily activities. Some areas were suggested under the section earlier on Cost Control. Others might include
Work flow
— have you done work-flow charting for all activities?
— where are the bottlenecks or impediments?
— what improvements are possible?
Buildings and accommodation
— do you know what these cost?
— how might better use be made of the space?
Plant and equipment
— would better training produce better results?
— would hiring or subcontracting out be more economical?
Transport
— how might costs be reduced?
Energy
— what are these costs?

— a study of energy management techniques could produce significant savings

And looking still wider
**Benchmarking** offers high potential for increased effectiveness.
This means studying organisations and activities in fields similar to your own to compare, evaluate and incorporate their best practices into your activities, measuring their performance against yours.

Organisations which do not maintain continuous improvement will fall behind in the marketplace. This is a race which has no finish line, and one in which you as a supervisor have an important contribution to make.
Initially you should ensure that each of your people becomes skilled in problem-solving techniques.

## RECORDS AND REPORTS                                      69

**Records** not only provide information for reports but are essential for planning and forecasting. So they must be up-to-date and accurate. The reason for keeping them should be clearly understood by those involved, because unless they are seen to be necessary they won't be taken seriously. Then the accuracy and the regularity of recording will suffer.
In general, records must be maintained for

* Information or reference purposes, e.g. personnel data such as home addresses
* Information for decision making by management, e.g. figures on production or costing or the building of a data base
* Information required by law, e.g. accident statistics.

Keep your records on properly prepared and headed books, forms or discs. You should not have to copy from scraps of paper. The first recording should be all that is needed, and if this is not now the case, talk to your manager about changing the procedure.

**Reports** are part of the communication system which binds the organisation together. Writing them may be part of your job so you should know what is required. A form with the various subject headings or questions already printed on it is very useful for regular reports following a set pattern. It gives the information in a standard layout which is easily read, referred to and compared with previous reports. The standard form could apply to reports dealing with production, sales, maintenance, accidents, in fact, to most things.

But occasionally you may have to write a special report on a particular subject. How well your report is written may determine whether or not your recommendations are accepted.

It should probably follow this pattern (number the paragraphs for ease of reference)

(a) Terms of reference — which show why you are writing the report
(b) An introductory paragraph — which states the problem and how it arose
(c) The body of the report — which sets out all the facts to be considered
(d) The conclusions you have reached
(e) Your recommendation.

People tend to act for one of two reasons
    to gain benefit, or
    to avoid loss.

The person who approves your recommendation will have the same motivation. Keep this in mind when formulating your conclusions. **A suggested check list for report writing is**

1 State the problem:
    — have you identified your purpose and your plan?
2 Collect and select your material:
    — does it all relate to the subject?
    — is it accurate?
    — have you distinguished between facts and opinions?
    — have you misstated or exaggerated anything?
    — have you omitted anything because it does not support your personal views? — a very real trap.
3 Arrange your material:
    — is the information clear, logical and self-explanatory?
    — do you show possible alternative lines of action?
4 Recommend:
    — be simple, clear and logical.
5 Re-check the report:
    — if you now saw it for the first time would the recommendation convince you? Why?

With so many other things happening it is not unusual for reports to be put to one side and action deferred. There are ways to break through this barrier

• Attach to your report an action plan showing how your recommendation can be implemented

- Ensure that the person who must approve it is not required to do any more than to say 'yes'
- Within ten days of submitting it make an appointment to call on this person to discuss your proposal and if possible then to produce some further supporting evidence.

---

Every record and every regular report should be challenged at least once a year.

- What does it achieve?
- Is it still necessary
  — in that format?
  — with that frequency?
- What would suffer if it were terminated?
- How could it be simplified?

---

# CHAPTER 6

# PEOPLE AT WORK

Before people can be expected to contribute they need to know what is the objective and its outcomes. They want to know what to do and how to do it.

They must be able to do it. They must want to do it.

They want to be kept informed and to be listened to, and they want appropriate recognition.

# SELECTING AND INTRODUCING THE NEW EMPLOYEE

## Selection*

Are you quite sure you need another person, or can the jobs be rearranged or reallocated? Will the total cost of employing another person be fully warranted by the work output? These are points on which you may have to convince your manager.

You should regard each vacancy to be filled as an investment opportunity and be aware that your appointee may be expected to move later to other positions within the organisation.

If it is necessary to recruit a new person for your unit the first step is to prepare a **Job Analysis** which studies both the job that has to be done (the job description) and the profile of your preferred appointee (the person specification). For instance:

- Is the Job Description up-to-date?
- Is any special skill or knowledge needed to do this work?
- Must the appointee have this skill or can it be taught on the job?
- Are there any physical requirements, e.g. colour vision, manual dexterity, mobility?
- Will the appointee be a member of a group, a lone worker, have contact with the public?
- What previous experience, if any, is desirable or necessary?
- What personal factors are important in this job? For instance:
  — communication skills
  — computer literacy
  — creativity and innovation
  — problem-solving ability
  — teamwork skills.

Then you should identify the **critical factors** which the appointee must have if he or she is to meet your performance expectations (these will probably not exceed seven). If any of these is missing in your best applicant you have three options

- To appoint and hope for success (experience suggests you won't get it because of the missing factor)
- To readvertise
- To restructure the job to suit the qualities of your best applicant.

When you are interviewing you should seek evidence of competency in each of the critical factors — for if you make a bad appointment training will not compensate and the effectiveness of your work group will be diminished. (And their effectiveness is your reputation.)

73

* This is described in more depth in *Selecting the Best* by Gordon P Rabey, also published by Longman Paul.

You may or may not participate in the initial interviewing of the applicants — often management or the personnel people handle this — but you should discuss with your manager the necessity for you to be involved in the final selection. The appointee will be a member of your work group and it is most important that he or she will fit in with you and your employees.

### There are three key questions in selection

- Can this person do the job? (covering knowledge and skill)
- Will this person do the job? (covering motivation)
- Will this person fit in with our work group? (covering personality and giving due regard to the culture of your organisation)

The selection interview should be so designed that each of these three areas is explored with care and this will mean asking planned open-ended questions to evoke facts and feelings on each. This will take time and thought.

In the identification of knowledge and skill acquired it must be recognised that this will apply not only to that gained in academic or employment situations. People gain knowledge and skills in a wide variety of situations, paid and unpaid, and this should not be overlooked in assessing competency. This background is usually recorded as recognition of prior learning (RPL).

In the formal offer of appointment the person being appointed should be told what he or she will be required to do and the conditions of employment which should be confirmed in writing. Any subsequent change in those conditions may need to be renegotiated.

You should be aware, of course, that unless there are very special circumstances you cannot discriminate against applicants on the basis of sex, ethnic origins or religious beliefs and that the principles of equal employment opportunity must be observed.

## Introducing the New Employee

Do you remember your first day at work, when there was you, all alone, and 'them', who was everyone else? And how long it took to change to thinking about the people around you as 'we'.

Things haven't changed. The new employee still feels out of things, a little confused, and perhaps even unwanted.

**First impressions can't be postponed** so the first two or three weeks are critical. In this time the new employee has to become part of your work group. This means that he or she must have

— a clearly defined job, a job to be regarded as one's own and for which there will be a personal responsibility
— a job which keeps one fully occupied and which is known to have a real purpose

— a proper work place and work layout safely run
— a work routine and good instructions which will lead to full competence
— wages which are felt to be fair for the work done
— recognition as a person
— a feeling of belonging in the work group
— information on all relevant matters
— a clear source of authority
— opportunity to do one's best and to fully use skill and knowledge.

If the new employees feel they are not getting these things they will probably leave. If they stay they could become either employees with problems or problem employees — in either case your team will suffer.

There are six steps in the right way to start the new employees (sometimes called **induction training**)

*Step 1 — Establish a friendly contact*
— greet them cordially and put at ease
— show a sincere interest in each of them
— explain the functions of the organisation and of your particular group and the opportunities for advancement
— outline their particular duties and responsibilities.

*Step 2 — Explain important rules and regulations*
— attendance rules and records
— safety practices
— special rules and perhaps legal requirements about the work of the unit
— union obligations.

*Step 3 — Explain the pay and the holiday procedures*
— the pay rate
— how, when and where it will be paid
— deductions and overtime
— holiday entitlements.

*Step 4 — Introduce them to the work place*
— be sure the work place is ready
— introduce them to fellow employees
— choose the right person to instruct
— give each a sketch floor plan showing where key people and places are.

*Step 5 — Put them to work and make sure they know*
— what to do and why it is needed
— what standards must be maintained
— where the work comes from
— where it goes to
— they are fully and gainfully employed (for confidence building their first jobs should be a success).

*Step 6 — Check back often to ensure that they*
— have been properly trained

— are fully occupied and competent
— are fully accepted as members of the group.

You may not do each of these things yourself, but if they are listed on a check sheet each step can be marked off as it is completed. You should ask the new employees to sign it to make sure that they too feel that everything has been covered.

Research shows that if new employees are properly introduced to the job, as described here, they are more likely to stay, and to be effective.

When a person leaves and has to be replaced it has been estimated that the total cost of this replacement (loss of production, recruitment costs, training, supervision, etc.) will be some 60 per cent of the annual pay for that position. Across an organisation that's a lot of money.

## SKILLS TRAINING

You are in charge of your unit; therefore, you are responsible for ensuring that each person in it receives proper and adequate training to do the work for which he or she is employed and also for future tasks which can be expected.

This means that you must be alert to identify and to record areas of work or people where or for whom you think training is needed. Then in discussion with your manager it can be decided whether you should do this training yourself or whether specialist assistance should be sought (perhaps by a training officer or through an Industry Training Board or at a Polytechnic or its equivalent).

As has been stated earlier your effectiveness is determined largely by the effectiveness of those who work for you; therefore, they must be capable and their training must be so planned that the potential of each person is developed and has the opportunity to be developed.

Good training will
— have specific learning and competency objectives
— be relevant to those involved
— be geared to their individual abilities and needs
— be regularly assessed to ensure it is accomplishing what it set out to do
— be maintained to meet other emerging needs.

In simple terms training comprises explanation, demonstration, imitation and application, but it has many other elements.

Training has three objectives

- To get work done (which is why people are employed)
- To develop people to meet the foreseeable needs of the organisation
- To seek to identify the potential that individuals have and to help them achieve it.

But **training** may be defined as putting knowledge and skill into people so that they may perform competently assigned tasks, and which must be maintained by the further input of reinforcement and coaching. **Learning,** however, is knowledge and skill drawn in by people who feel the need to acquire and retain it.

*One is reminded of an earlier 'Peanuts' cartoon in which one small boy says 'I have taught my dog to whistle'. The second small boy bends down to listen and says 'I can't hear anything' — to which the first one replies 'I said I have taught him to whistle — I didn't say he can whistle'.*

The difference between being trained and in seeking learning will blur when one takes personal ownership of the training process. Some organisations who recognise this are saying to staff

'We have agreed your work objectives for the coming year and you know that your performance will be reflected in salary recognition — now tell us what training you will need to help you achieve your targets' or 'If you're not prepared to invest in your own career why should we? Your future is in your hands.'

Supervisors should seek every opportunity to create learning situations, to encourage people to seek attendance at courses, to undertake study programmes, to ask for training, to challenge people to find solutions to problems. Perhaps organisations should stop running training courses and replace them with Learning Workshops. The term **Work Based Learning** is gaining wider recognition. It has been defined as 'A structured and integrated learning approach which incorporates both off and on the job learning to meet both organisation and individual goals.' One concern which initiated this concept is the perceived mismatch between a large unskilled work force and the growing complexity of task activities. The approach envisages individual development linking planned work place experience, on the job learning, off-job learning, and incorporates due recognition of prior learning (RPL). It requires employers and educational institutions to come together in a new relationship which will be reflected in the development of individually owned learning programmes. Work based learning is in its formative stages but it carries the seeds which may significantly change the traditional approaches to training.

One other definition is important: Skill and knowledge generated by training or learning situations, and which can be measured, is **ability**.

The application of this ability in the work place environment, and which is assessed and evaluated there, is **competency**. These two should not be confused.

Training can either be unplanned — a sort of 'watch me and try and pick it up' approach — or it can be planned. Both will cost money, but one will be much cheaper yet more effective.

Suppose the new employee is paid $450 per week and it takes three weeks to learn the job, in an unplanned and casual way:

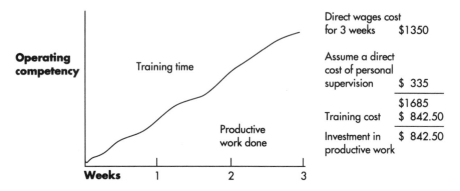

| | |
|---|---|
| Direct wages cost for 3 weeks | $1350 |
| Assume a direct cost of personal supervision | $ 335 |
| | $1685 |
| Training cost | $ 842.50 |
| Investment in productive work | $ 842.50 |

but suppose that with planned systematic training the new employee can operate competently with minimum supervision within one week:

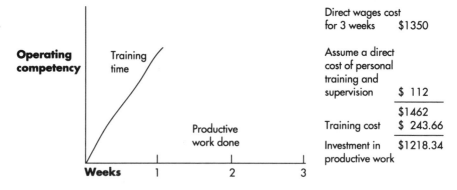

| | |
|---|---|
| Direct wages cost for 3 weeks | $1350 |
| Assume a direct cost of personal training and supervision | $ 112 |
| | $1462 |
| Training cost | $ 243.66 |
| Investment in productive work | $1218.34 |

Thus, in this example planned training would give you $375.84 more investment in productive work and the need for less close supervision in the first three weeks. So without it costing more than in the previous method you could spend up to $598.84 (i.e. $842.50 – $243.66 on the special training **of this one person**. The shorter the time of systematic training the greater the saving.

## What is planned training?

There are four stages:
**1  Determine what is to be taught and what standard of ability is expected**

To take an example below from a highly skilled workshop task, for each skill level a specific performance standard would be defined and training be geared to produce that standard. Wage differentials may also be related to these skill levels.

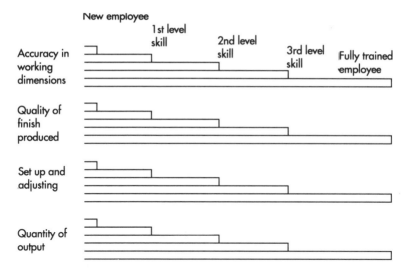

Another method of analysis is to take a specific job, break it down into its component parts, and then decide how much skill is needed for each part

0 indicating no knowledge or skill required
1 indicating some knowledge or skill required
2 indicating good knowledge or skill required
3 indicating full and detailed knowledge or skill required.
e.g. A task in the construction industry:

| Task Concreting form work | | Unskilled employees | Skilled employees | Leading hand | Supervisor | Overseer |
|---|---|---|---|---|---|---|
| Parts of | A | 1 | 2 | 2 | 3 | 3 |
| this | B | 0 | 0 | 1 | 2 | 3 |
| operation | C | 0 | 2 | 3 | 3 | 3 |
| | D | 1 | 1 | 2 | 3 | 3 |
| | E | 1 | 2 | 2 | 3 | 3 |

This analysis of the jobs shows the level of skill and knowledge which must be taught to each group at each stage of the processing or operation. Then by using the capability chart described earlier individual training needs may be identified.

## 2 Teach the skill required

Training may be given on or off the job, in Polytechnics or equivalent, in special training areas, in groups or individually — but, wherever and however it is done, you, the supervisor, must be concerned with it and be

79

fully informed. Whatever is taught, you will supervise the application of the skill to the task, and you are responsible for the results.

Most training is given on the job.

One method discussed here uses the **Work Sheet** (or the Job Breakdown).

A Work Sheet is a listing of the separate steps, in logical sequence, which make up a particular job. It defines a standard routine, and is widely accepted as being an invaluable teaching aid. It may be a supplementary sheet to a job description, or it may be held at the location where the job is done.

When Work Sheets are used

- Spoken instructions do not need frequent repetition
- Interruptions to the supervisor's own work are reduced
- Learning time is less
- Standardised methods are taught (Standard Operating Procedures — SOPs)
- Causes of error may be readily identified
- Each step of the job is taught separately and in the right order.

Work Sheets are set out in three matching parts
what has to be done
how to do it
why it should be done this way.

**Work sheet**

Task: to change a car wheel

| Main steps (What has to be done) | Key points (How to do it) | Reasons (Why it should be done this way) |
|---|---|---|
| 1  Switch off engine | Ignition switch | Safety |
| 2  Put into gear | 1st gear | To prevent car moving |
| 3  Block wheel | Rock or chock | To stop car sliding |
| 4  Take out tools | Check spare, jack, wheelbrace, screwdriver | |
| 5  Remove hubcap | With screwdriver | |
| 6  Loosen wheel nuts | One full turn | For easy removal when wheel off ground |
| / and so on / | | |

*Note*

- Each main step advances the job one stage
- Where the job carries any element of risk a further column 'Safety Factors' should be added
- If the work force is multicultural the Work Sheet may be prepared in the appropriate language
- Supporting diagrams, charts or 'exploded' drawings are often clearer than words
- Any routine task in any discipline can be taught by this method
- The starting point and the level of presentation should be geared to the level of the learner.

**How to teach a job by using a Work Sheet:**
You cannot do this just by giving a Work Sheet to an employee and expecting a faultless job. There must be proper training by a competent instructor. One proven method is

(a)  Create an interest in the job:
— be at ease yourself and put the learner at ease
— show why the job is important.
(b)  Explain the job:
— state what the job is
— find out what is known about it
— ensure the learner can watch you doing it.
(c)  Demonstrate the method:
— use a Work Sheet or other notes
— give the information logically, one step at a time
— stress the points to be watched
— take it easily, don't give more than can be absorbed
— seek questions
— do it again.
(d)  Assess performance:
— let the learner do the job, step by step (You can't teach a person by correspondence how to ride a bicycle)
— correct errors
— get it done again, the learner to explain at each step why it is being done that way (this is the key stage for it will demonstrate understanding)
— repeat until you know that the learner knows.
(e)  Review periodically and continue to coach on the job:
— put to work
— tell how to get help if needed
— check until you are both satisfied.

The word CEDAR will help you remember these five steps.

81

Each step is essential, and each must be completed before the next is started.

Instruction given on the job in this way in proper steps has proved to be effective across the world, but in each case the actual teaching must be geared to the employee concerned. No two people will learn in exactly the same way. For instance, older employees will relate their training to their previous experience, and to their previous social and working habits. Younger employees may need to be challenged to learn.

Learning by rote or by memorising is not always the best way. It may be better to encourage self-testing at each step so that the learner wants to progress to the next logical step.

Remember, too, that the new employee should start by reaching the standard of performance that is expected. Insist on this. Speed can be built up with practice, but standards seldom are. (*Note:* coaching which is the follow up is discussed in the next chapter.)

An example of a Work Sheet used by one organisation follows on page 83.

Reference is made above to 'a competent instructor'. This may not necessarily be the supervisor — it could be a skilled employee. But it presupposes that whoever does the training
— fully understands the job and knows the how and why of each job
— has the patience, tact and tolerance needed to teach it properly.

Usually the skills of this training can be gained in local short Instructor Training Courses of two or three days, or less.

As an alternative to the Work Sheet a **'Peat Sheet'** offers a simple approach. The example here deals with the display of stock in a supermarket:

**Purpose:**
- To attract the attention of the customer
- To promote a sale

**Equipment:**
Price marker, stock list, price tickets, trolley, stock

**Action:**
- Draw stock from store
- Ensure each item is correctly priced
- Fill display — stacked or tumbled
    old stock at front or on top
    labels to face customers
    remove any damaged stock

**Test:**
Customers can see easily and quickly
    what the goods are, what they offer, what they cost

# Skill training guide — worksheet

**Task :** _____
**Objective :** _____

**Unit :** _____

| What (Each step advances the job one stage) | How (Actions) | Why (Reason) |
|---|---|---|
| | | |

| Method | Feedback |
|---|---|
| **Preparation** | |
| • Tell job purpose | • Find out how much learner may know |
| **Demonstration** | |
| • Trainer demonstrates and explains **what-how-why** | • Learner observes |
| **Partial tryout** | |
| • Trainer does operation while learner explains **what-how-why** | • Trainer corrects errors in learner's explanation (if any) |
| **Complete tryout** | |
| • Learner demonstrates and explains **what-how-why** | • Trainer observes, questions and assists |
| **On job coaching** | |
| • Periodic checks | • Observation • Questions |

Another very effective training method is **Crisis Training**. Next time a crisis hits your work group deal with it as you usually do but as soon as things return to normal bring together the people who were involved in the situation and make time to discuss three questions

- What happened?
- What caused it?
- What we can learn from it?

Because the crisis is real the learning experience it creates has real significance, but it must lead in to action planning.

## 3 Evaluate the effectiveness of the training

Training costs money and you must satisfy yourself, and your manager, that it is meeting its objectives. Before any training starts it is essential that you are able to define clearly 'at the end of this training he/she should be competent to .........................'. If you can't do this with complete clarity should you proceed?

Evaluating the effectiveness of training is wholly dependent upon the precision of the definition of the training objectives.

After training you should discuss its effectiveness both with those involved and with your manager, not only so that the newly acquired skill or knowledge is being properly used but also to find out whether this training has, in fact, uncovered any other training needs. This happens quite often. You should have measurable criteria here.

The people concerned usually feel enthused by their training experience and you should try to encourage each to continue to seek additional knowledge and skill.

Consider your work group

- Who are your best employees?
  what makes them so? what does this tell you?
- Who are your least competent employees?
  can you devise a specific training and a coaching programme for each of them which will bring them up to a higher standard within, say, two months?

## 4 Maintain training records

Your organisation should have an established method of keeping training records and you must comply with this. However, there may be value in keeping a simple record of the training of people in your unit. This could be on individual cards as set out on the following page.

But concurrently with this you will also need to ensure that a record is maintained of

training courses attended or planned

training attachments or secondments.

| Name | | | Position:<br>Since: | | |
|---|---|---|---|---|---|
| Date | Training needed | Training given | Date | By | Assessment or achievement |
| | | | | | |

In many organisations this record is now incorporated into computerised Personnel Records and when this is done the information base can be expanded quite significantly.

Learning is the development of oneself and should be a life-long continuing process. The concept of **staircasing** or **articulation** enhances this through the assertion that no training course (or learning workshop) should be a dead end. Satisfactory completion to a predetermined standard should offer a credit or an exemption into a more advanced experience or a higher qualification.

To illustrate from one progression: short-course training in supervision is presented in three stages (A, B and C). The completion of these, plus linking work-based projects, will give subject exemptions towards a Certificate in Supervisory Management, leading into a Certificate of Management, then to a Management Diploma, to a graduate qualification, and perhaps in time to an MBA. This particular instance offers a good example of second-chance education.

Once an educational progression has been established stepping stones are in place, at which point each individual must decide how far along them he or she is prepared to advance. It's their future, it's their choice.

85

## COMMUNICATION

Communication means a transfer of meaning across a bridge of understanding.

Communication is reception — it is not transmission. The only message that passes is what the other person understands.

Your effectiveness as a supervisor, your effectiveness as a person will depend largely upon how well you communicate.

No matter what you know or how technically competent you are, your job is to get work done by others — and, therefore, you must be able to communicate effectively. And the message is not what you tell them, it is what they hear and understand. Therefore, you will need feedback to ensure that there is correct understanding, and this can be critical.

You are responsible for the effects of your communication, and if you are not getting the response you want perhaps you should change what you are doing.

Each person is a unique individual. Thus, when you want to get a person to do something or to change behaviour you must recognise this and gear your communication to trigger the reaction you seek.

86

Good communication will build continuing understanding between people. The criteria for good communication are

- Know what you want to say
- Transmit it in the most effective way
- Check that it was received and understood
- Listen for meanings.

Seek first to understand, and then to be understood.

The response will be related in some way to personality factors and to personal needs — for status, security, team membership, recognition as an individual, money, demonstration of competency, etc. We each have pressure points which will respond to stimulus.

There is never no communication — some message will be passing.

A high proportion of industrial disputes and stoppages, at least a third, are because of a breakdown in communication. Misunderstandings lead to confusion, mistakes, wastage and accidents, and raise barriers between people. Communication problems cause more difficulties for supervisors than almost anything else.

**Your relationships will be only as good as your communication.**

If your staff don't know management objectives how can they have any commitment to them?

If your staff don't know the progress being made towards the achievement of objectives why should they care?

'From where I sit' — is a phrase you should remember. We see any situation from the perspective of our background, position, experience, value systems and expectation — but others may perceive the same situation quite differently from their viewpoints. If you say 'From where I sit this is how I see it ......... Do you see it the same way?' a lot of misunderstanding and conflict would not arise.

Good communication will be

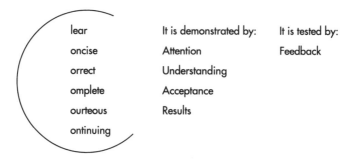

| | It is demonstrated by: | It is tested by: |
|---|---|---|
| lear | Attention | Feedback |
| oncise | Understanding | |
| orrect | Acceptance | |
| omplete | Results | |
| ourteous | | |
| ontinuing | | |

It is the bloodstream of every organisation.

As a supervisor you must
know the outcomes you want
notice the outcomes you're getting
adapt to the situation.

'I know that you believe you understand what you think I said, but I'm not sure you realise that what you heard is not what I meant.'
Have you ever been in this position?

Your responsibility for good communication is in four major directions
1 **To management** — decisions are made on the basis of known facts, and the manager expects to be kept fully informed by you on
— matters on which he or she must make reports or decisions
— matters which may cause controversy
— trends, attitudes and morale.

2 **To your employees** — they expect at all times to know about matters which will affect them and which interest them. Every employee is a public relations agent for the organisation and for your unit. They are part of it only as long as they feel they are. The need to know what is going on is important to each of us. Good communication is the bonding of teamwork.

3 **To your fellow supervisors** — your unit is part of a wider activity, and if the overall aims are to be reached all units must work in harmony and share information on both facts and trends.

4 **To clients, customers or the public** — they expect information associated with quality service which represents your organisation at its best. You're in the pivotal position here.

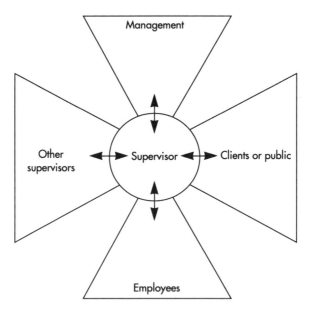

This carries with it considerable responsibility for not only must you pass on factual information, ideas and indicators of feelings but also because of your intermediary role you may either consciously or subconsciously filter these communications so that the message being passed may become distorted, abbreviated or enlarged. And the outcome may not be what was intended.

## Listening

But at the same time, management, your employees and your fellow supervisors will be communicating with you on all of these things and your job is to listen. This is not easy

- Don't interrupt
- Don't assume anything
- Try to understand the reason behind the message
- Ask questions to make the meaning clearer
- Don't react too quickly
- Get all the information. Don't feel 'I've made up my mind; therefore, more facts will confuse me.'

Listening is wanting to hear.

Listening is the beginning of understanding. Not everyone is fluent in speaking or writing and words are just clues to the real message. Listening is an active process. It means

- Hearing
- Interpreting
- Evaluating
- Responding.

Good listening is not critical of the speaker or the message. It is not judgemental. It will be most effective and powerful when it is reflective listening.

Reflective listening will reduce conflict, lower tension and significantly assist people to resolve their own situations. In reflective listening the listener restates briefly the feeling and/or the content of what has been said and does it in such a way that demonstrates understanding and acceptance.

For instance, 'You were enjoying it. Then things started to go wrong and this made you angry?'

This encourages the speaker to continue and the feedback gives a pause to reflect on what has been said and on its implications. The listener does not attempt to lead the discussion nor to divert it but to seek clarification of the real issues, to encourage the speaker to get beneath the symptoms to the causes and then to develop a constructive reaction.

This skill takes practice but it's worth it. Start perhaps in your listening by thinking 'If I were having that experience how would I be feeling?'

Good listeners are very popular people, because there are so few of them.

A very good guideline here is: treat your staff as if they were working for you voluntarily. Then you'll listen to them.

The goal of listening is to understand the content of the other person's ideas or proposals, the meaning it has for him or her, and the feelings he or she has about it.

You
must
communicate with

Management    Your          Your          Other units
              work group    clients

But, just as importantly, they
will communicate with you,
and

You must listen

'We do not understand an opposing idea until we have so exposed
ourselves to it that we feel the pull of its persuasion, until we
arrive at the point where we really see the power of whatever
element of truth it contains.'

Reasonable people will usually agree with each other if they know
clearly what they are talking about. They take care to prevent barriers
between them which might distort the meaning of the message.

The tone of your voice is important here. If you were to ask someone
'What are you doing?' you should get a straightforward reply. But if you
were to say 'What *are* you doing?' the other person will think you are being
sarcastic and will react to your sarcasm before he or she even considers
the question.

When next you encounter or become involved in a people-problem
look first for a human misunderstanding, a breakdown in communication.
You will almost certainly find the cause.

Listening often requires asking questions to seek clarity. People tend to
generalise and to avoid the specific, using words like 'always', 'never',
'everyone'. Challenge these by asking 'always?', 'never?', 'everyone?', and
with questions such as 'Who said so?', 'What was actually said?', 'What
was meant?', 'How was it known?' If you don't do this you too could pass
on incomplete or distorted information. Generalisations indicate sloppy
thinking.

## Staff Meetings

It is becoming common practice now to hold five-minute staff meetings
at the start of each day to discuss topics such as yesterday's highlights,
today's requirements, other matters of interest, and to listen to each other.

Whether it is planned or not communication will inevitably be a topic of discussion at your own staff meetings. To stimulate thinking you should explore sources of communication breakdown:

1   Ask 'Where are we having communication problems with others and what can be done to resolve them?'

**Towards improved communication**

| Recommendation | This would achieve | Action should be initiated by |
|---|---|---|
| | | |

2   Ask 'What communication problems do we have in our own activities?'

| There was a communication breakdown when | This was probably caused by | It could have been prevented if |
|---|---|---|
| | | |

## Management information systems

If you are to function effectively have you identified

- What information you must have?
- How often you must have it?
- What form it should take?
- How you will use it?

Do you receive it?

91

There are two major divisions:

| Planning information | Control information |
|---|---|
| Crosses over organisational lines | Follows organisational lines |
| Shows trends: long-time periods | Short-time periods |
| Non-financial data important | Non-financial data important |
| Lacks minute detail | Very detailed |
| Future oriented | Historically oriented |

But with so much data now being fed into computers and processed into printouts an emerging problem is information overload.

You need to separate a feeling of wonder at what today's computers can do from a realistic look at whether or not this technology is doing the maximum to make your job easier and you more effective. Data processing people should be studying your needs and devising the most cost-effective ways of meeting them. If this is not already happening you should ask for such a study. You want accurate and timely simplicity, not complexity.

## Public Relations

**Communication — your Public Relations**

- Do you know what your employees think about the organisation?
    how do you know?
    does it matter what they think?
- Do your employees know what the objectives are?
    have they accepted these as their own objectives, either in whole or in part?
- Do you know what your employees want to know?
    do you tell them these things?
    what happens then?
- In terms of objectives and their achievement how well informed are your:
    customers or clients?
    shareholders or public?
- How do you know the effectiveness of your
    telephone, reception and counter service? and
    is it just as good when relieving staff are on duty?

Remember: your dissatisfied employees, customers or clients are your Public Relations people in your community. Research has shown that a satisfied person may tell one other person
    — a dissatisfied one will tell at least eleven others

## Networking

Information is power. In your job you should be building and maintaining a network of personal contacts in your and related fields of interest, both nationally and internationally. You need to keep up with technology and its applications, to exchange information. If you read an article which impresses you say so in a letter to the writer — you'll usually get a response.

For people planning advancement networking is now regarded as indispensable.

## Negotiating

(This refers here to an aspect of everyday communication, not to the more legalistic components of industrial relations.)

Negotiation means conferring with another for the purpose of arranging some matter by mutual agreement. It is a process of influencing behaviour, a method whereby parties who may have conflicting aims establish the terms on which they will co-operate.

Success depends upon these things

93

- The issue is negotiable
- The negotiators are able to exchange value for value
- To a degree the parties trust each other.

In every negotiation certain elements are present and it is important that each party identifies what the other's position is regarding

- Key objectives
- Information — both facts and needs
- Time — deadlines
- Power — who has it — who makes the decisions.

All parties in a negotiation should come out with some needs satisfied. The aim should be a co-operative win-win. If the outcome is win-lose, it is likely that the issue has not been resolved and that next time it will be more difficult.

Your first step is to identify your objective. In this you should distinguish between your absolute requirements and your desirable targets — the latter are your bargaining areas but the former may need redefinition during the negotiation.

Four basic strategies are common to most negotiations once the objective has been decided

1 **People** — separate the person from the problem. If you attack the person emotions will be aroused and the real issue will become submerged and blurred.

2 **Interests** — focus on interests not on positions. Identify interests which define the problem and concentrate on information relating to them. Seek data which will give you leverage. Both parties may not have the same interests.

3 **Options** — generate as many options as possible before deciding what to do. Identify the differences between you for these may point the way to a solution.

4 **Criteria** — commit yourself to a solution based on principle, not pressure.

The tactic is collaborative problem solving.

Good negotiating requires considerable skill — if your job requires it you should seek training and coaching in its strategy and tactics. This is recommended for many life situations require negotiating ability.

## Team Briefing

Team briefing is a system of planned meetings to pass on factual information from management to staff and from staff to management. Its aim is to be fast and accurate and to beat the grapevine. If appropriate these meetings should involve everybody and be held regularly. Monthly is recommended. The time should not exceed 30 minutes.

The information should be concerned with current activity, projected activity, policy, people and points for action.

The concept is that at a top level management meeting a decision is made on what information should be passed down. Each senior manager then uses this as an agenda for discussion with his or her managers, each of whom then holds meetings with their supervisors who in turn meet with employees, and similarly their responses are fed back up. At each stage other relevant material can be included.

The concept is good but for team briefing to be successful continuing top level support and commitment is essential and the use of a facilitator may be necessary to ensure that the system operates as planned.

Other difficulties are a tendency for managers to filter out information they do not wish to pass on, and the lack of suitable processes to feed information back up to top levels.

If a team briefing system is not operating where you work your people will expect you to be their source of information.

---

**Better communication**

- Do I know precisely what I want to communicate?
- What do I expect to happen when my message has been passed?
- What other interpretations might be put on my message? Can I be misunderstood — and, if so, how can I prevent this?

- Is my message complete, correct and appropriate to the situation under review? Do I tell people what they need to know?
- What feedback will I get to test the effectiveness of the communication?
- Do I really listen to people?
  How do I know this?
- What communication breakdown have I experienced today? Why did it happen? Can it happen again?

Good communication is the life-blood of teamwork.

When I communicate I am wholly responsible for the outcome.

If a message can be understood in different ways it will be understood in just that way which does the most harm.

## PERFORMANCE APPRAISAL

Performance appraisal should be concerned with

95

- Strengthening the organisation
- Appraising present performance matched with agreed objectives
- Developing people to meet future organisational needs
- Helping each person to develop potential
- Responding to two questions which everyone has
  'How well am I performing?'
  'Where can I go from here?'

How this is done will vary from organisation to organisation. Some tend to overlook that 60 per cent of the word appraisal is 'praise'.

There is a measure of misunderstanding about appraisals and performance reviews. For some it is a once a year assessment of performance under generalised headings. For others, more realistically, it is an annual attempt to evaluate actual performance against personal or unit objectives set at the beginning of the year, and which have been reviewed regularly in the interim.

But it should be more than this. In many cases the objective of appraisal needs to be redefined

- Is it a control mechanism to secure sustained output (summative appraisal)?
- Is it a process for individual development (formative appraisal)?
- Is it designed to coach and encourage a winning team leader or team member?

It is important to establish whether it is seen by staff to be threatening or challenging for they will react accordingly.

After appraisal is there a planned and systematic follow-up which is subsequently evaluated?

The following four-step approach outlines one method of performance appraisal you may find appropriate:

1  The individual discusses his or her job description with the immediate supervisor or manager and they agree on the

   • key tasks
   • areas of accountability
   • specific objectives and output targets for the forthcoming year.

2  Checkpoints and dates are established for regular evaluation of progress. As stated earlier, change is happening so quickly today that every objective should be systematically reviewed at least every 90 days. Few will stay completely unchanged for a year.

3  Coaching, discussion and encouragement should be maintained throughout the year. There should be informal meetings for this purpose with each person at least monthly. In the end of year appraisal there should be no surprises.

4  At the annual appraisal discussion self-appraisal should be one facet of it and the review should cover achievements and their components matched with targets, problems encountered and how resolved, any training or other need emerging, special factors, and conclude with a specific commitment to ongoing action geared to identified needs. This will emerge from a collaborative solution seeking and planning approach in a relaxed atmosphere. This means that both of you should have adequate time to prepare for this meeting, and you should do a lot of listening.

You should direct the discussion into the key results areas of the job (usually called KRA) as defined in the Job Description. These could cover, for instance

• quantity and quality of output
• customer focus
• cost-effectiveness or achievements within budgets
• interactive relationships
• people management and team building
• utilisation of resources including time management
• paper work and communication
• personal growth.

To establish talking points you might individually score each of these headings on a scale and then discuss any significant differences. You should consider areas of success and of problems, likes and dislikes, dealing with each constructively.

The outcome should be to enable each individual to see the job in its organisational perspective, to identify areas for personal growth or improvement, to translate these into action plans and to carry them through to results.

For the organisation one key objective must be to ensure that an adequate return is being gained on the investment in salaries and wages.

97

*Team performance appraisal*

With the emphasis now on team building and team development there should also be a process of team performance appraisal. The pattern outlined above would be appropriate.

*Appraisal for promotion*

This should be based on different criteria for it has a different objective. The person should have had opportunities to demonstrate potential — through the performance of delegated tasks, leading small projects, deputising for a senior, etc — and the appraisal should be linked to these. Outstanding performance on present duties is not in itself an indicator of suitability for promotion to other duties. The next level of advancement may require quite different skills, behaviour and knowledge and to promote someone beyond their achievable ability can both destroy the individual and impair the effectiveness of the organisation. Seeking and gaining appropriate qualifications can be a factor here.

## GIVING INSTRUCTIONS

Every instruction you give carries with it the danger of ambiguity

• what you think you said

- what you actually said
- what the other person thinks you said.

This shows up in what then happens. And if it is not what you intended the fault is probably yours.

Before you give an instruction

- be sure you have your facts right — all of them
- can it be interpreted in ways other than the way you intend? If it can be, it will be
- in this situation how important is feedback?
- is the instruction in every way appropriate to the situation?

How an instruction is given will depend upon the situation and the person and this can range from a direct command through to a request for volunteers. Good instruction will have identifiable characteristics

- compatible with objectives — it makes sense
- reasonable — achievable. Resources are available. Timing is adequate
- intelligible — the terms and the words are understandable. If necessary this should be tested by feedback
- appropriate — the wording (instruction, request, etc.) is appropriate to the situation
- respect — respect is mutual.

Instructions should be in writing if they

- are complex
- assign specific accountability
- are to continue beyond the present situation
- are necessary for a particular individual or situation.

But they should be clear and unambiguous. Check this by discussion to ensure that the message is clearly understood.

A **command** or a direct order is one-way communication to get a quick response and its meaning must be quite clear. Much depends on the tone of voice, but properly used and where reasons for it are obvious, it usually works. But a sensitive person might be antagonised by it.

A **request** is more personal and tactful and seeks co-operation. It is particularly useful when dealing with older or experienced employees or with people who lack confidence.

The **suggestion** is a mild request, open to refusal. Limit its use to the reliable and experienced employees or to occasions when you want to stimulate initiative.

**Asking for volunteers** may be useful if the task is particularly difficult or perhaps unpleasant or where it is not appropriate to specifically name one person. If morale is low no one may respond.

As a simple yardstick, ask yourself 'What kind of orders or instructions do I dislike getting?' Be guided by your own feelings and experience.

## EMPLOYEE RELATIONS

Usually employee relations denotes the relationships between employers and employees in all work situations relating to conditions of employment which are or may be covered by awards or agreements.

To the supervisor this means that the dealings with employees in every situation must be seen to be fair and be felt to be fair. And the local union representative has the same responsibility.

Both should also have a real concern for the economic viability of the organisation. Samuel Gompers, a prominent US union official, once said 'The greatest disservice a company can do to workers is to run an unprofitable operation.'

So, you and the union representative should have much in common. As far as it is appropriate — and your manager should guide you in this — you should

- pass on factual information — this will kill rumours and beat the grapevine
- consult on such things as pending changes
- be well briefed on all the conditions of employment relating to your work group, on the appropriate award, and on legislation which concerns your activities
- ensure that you are the first contact regarding complaints and grievances
- know clearly how to handle disciplinary matters.

The union representative speaks on behalf of the members and has a position of influence. You, the supervisor, have assigned responsibility and authority but even so you too are to a degree dependent upon your influence with the group.

Perhaps the most significant point your manager must recognise is that you must be kept fully informed at all times — for **if the union representative knows more than you who then leads the group**?

This is a sensitive area. Both unions and management are seen to be competing for the loyalty of the employees but it should not be a conflict situation. To your employees you represent management, to management you represent the employees for whom you are the team leader. And in your pivot role you have to be scrupulously honest, consistent and sincere in the balancing of your responsibilities.

99

# HANDLING COMPLAINTS AND GRIEVANCES

A grievance is any situation or act which is unfair in the mind of the complainer. An imagined grievance is a grievance.

Most fires can be put out with a teacup full of water applied at the right time and place. Take care of the small problems and the larger ones may never develop.

You should distinguish between on-job and off-job causes.

Of the on-job causes it has been said that most grievances arise from lack of understanding of the purposes behind various regulations and orders issued by management representatives. Other causes may lie within areas of control or communication. A check sheet on these three points for analysis by supervisors is shown on page 101.

Still further causes will be favouritism in assigning work, credit-stealing, favouritism in promotion, lack of supervisor's interest in work or employees, and no doubt others will come to mind.

Under the heading of off-job causes would be

- housing difficulties
- domestic troubles
- financial problems
- personal disturbances.

But if one of your staff has such a problem, to what extent should you become involved in it? The answer must be that if it interferes in any way with work output or performance you cannot ignore it.

## The Effects of Grievances

Partly handled or neglected grievances invariably produce very serious effects. For instance

- disgruntled employees are less efficient
- an employee with an unsettled grievance spreads dissatisfaction to other employees
- an unsettled grievance may cause the loss of a good employee
- an employee concerned about a grievance becomes a greater safety risk
- overall efficiency is reduced by an unsettled grievance.

So you must act quickly before the situation becomes aggravated and a minor complaint escalates into a major disturbance of rapidly increasing complexity. You will not often achieve a satisfactory solution by telling the employee to 'forget it'.

Surveys have indicated that most grievances originate in one of these areas

- hours and pay
- responsibility and authority
- supervision
- work flow

- working conditions
    light, ventilation, dirt,
    noise, temperature,
    materials, etc.
- fatigue
- communication breakdown

- work layout
- transportation
- social contact
- monotony, boredom
- advancement prospects
- planning defects.

Which of these could be breeding a grievance in your work group right now?

---

**A check sheet to assist in detecting some causes of grievances**
It has been said that most grievances arise from lack of an understanding of the purposes behind the various regulations and orders issued by representatives of management.

The following questions are designed to identify possible sources of misunderstanding in your unit.

**Regulations**

|  | Yes | No |
|---|---|---|
| Does any regulation by which you control your employees irritate them by implying that you do not trust them? | ☐ | ☐ |
| Does any regulation cause hardship on many in order to control a few? | ☐ | ☐ |
| Does any regulation carry a threat that would be embarrassing to enforce? | ☐ | ☐ |
| Is there any rule that is not absolutely necessary? | ☐ | ☐ |
| Can you guarantee that each employee knows why each regulation is necessary? | ☐ | ☐ |
| Does any rule in your unit set up stricter control than that in other departments? | ☐ | ☐ |
| Do you maintain any rule which is considered by the employees to be unfair? | ☐ | ☐ |

**Control**

|  | Yes | No |
|---|---|---|
| Do you make it a point to get all the facts before you reprimand an employee? | ☐ | ☐ |
| Do you take care that all reprimands to an employee are made in private? | ☐ | ☐ |
| Is any employee handicapped by your poor enforcement of discipline? | ☐ | ☐ |
| Do you make certain that no employee is subjected to constant annoyance, either oral or physical, by other employees? | ☐ | ☐ |
| Are the earnings of every employee fair in comparison with the earnings of others doing work of equal value or requiring equal skill? | ☐ | ☐ |
| Is there any operation which is not as safe as it could be made? | ☐ | ☐ |

**Communication**

|  | Yes | No |
|---|---|---|
| Do your employees talk to you as freely as you would wish? | ☐ | ☐ |
| Could any employee complain that he or she has not had adequate instruction? | ☐ | ☐ |
| Do you pass on at once any information given you for distribution? | ☐ | ☐ |
| Do employees believe that their suggestions are handled fairly and impartially? | ☐ | ☐ |
| Think carefully — have you made any promise to any employee that has not been fulfilled? | ☐ | ☐ |
| Do you make a habit of answering the questions of the employees as promptly and completely as possible? | ☐ | ☐ |

**Action needed:**

Many organisations still have instructions or regulations on their books which were relevant and appropriate when first issued but which are now obsolete. They should be purged for their existence can generate problems.

If you have an Employee Relations Officer seek advice before taking action. There may be precedents for this incident or hidden agenda items.

**To handle a grievance properly there are four key steps**

1  Listen with an open mind

- listen patiently, even if the grievance appears minor
- be sure you get the whole story
- probe gently: ask 'why do you think that?' or 'why do you think it happened that way?'
- discuss but do not argue
- look for the main symptoms — these are not necessarily the first or the most obvious
- note, however, the grievance may not be expressed only in words.

2  Get all the facts straight (your diagnosis)

- encourage a restatement of the grievance
- question carefully and try to distinguish between facts and opinions
- talk to others, or consult records, if necessary
- if need be, discuss the situation with your superiors
- don't jump to conclusions
- check every angle of the complaint. Do any recent cases or happenings have a bearing on the matter?
- check policy. See how the complaint affects present practices, interpretations or policies. Is there any precedent?
- examine the employee's record. What is the work history and disciplinary record? Is he or she usually dependable and stable?

3  Act promptly and fairly

- first, ask
  — is this my responsibility?
  — do I have authority to take action?
  — can I handle it myself? or
  — what do I recommend?
- then
  — discuss with the union delegate, if necessary, and if you are authorised to do so
  — don't delay action or pass the buck if it's within your power to do something

— try to save face — you should not reduce the person's dignity
— if you cannot give a decision say so, and why. If you report it up-
   wards, give all the facts, not just the ones that support your views
— if your answer is 'no', give reasons
— be ready to give the benefit of the doubt
— don't use your authority to force a decision
— don't act impetuously; think not only what you will do but also
   about the likely consequences
— state when a decision may be expected.

*Note:* You must be aware of the grievance procedures described in the
employee relations legislation. This will outline your specific responsibilities and obligations. You should discuss this with your manager to
ascertain whether there are also any local interpretations of which you
should be aware.

The usual practice is

- The grievance must first be discussed with the immediate supervisor
- If it cannot be resolved satisfactorily at that level it should be
  referred to the manager to whom the supervisor reports. The union
  representative may become involved at this point
- If no satisfactory decision is then reached the issue may be referred
  by written submissions to a grievance committee comprising representatives for both the employer and the union with an independent
  chairperson. The decision at this point is usually binding on both
  parties.

103

4  Follow-up

- to ensure that the action taken was correct and that you dealt with
  causes, not just the effects
- report to your manager all major grievances you settle satisfactorily
  as well as the ones where you consult others. You may be setting a
  precedent
- maintain a summary record of the grievances you handle.

It has been suggested that a competent supervisor should be able to
resolve the greater majority of grievances which arise in the work group if
the guidelines are followed.

Grievances may test your relationships with shop stewards or union
delegates. You both have a job to do and a hard line is often not the best
approach. A frank discussion seeking facts, free from emotional overtones,
and handled quietly, will gain respect and usually will produce good
results. You should ensure that your actions will cast light and not heat on
problem situations.

## DEALING WITH CONFLICT

A conflict is a situation in which two or more people desire goals which they perceive as being attainable by one or the other but not by both. Sometimes it can be described as a clash of opposing emotions.

To be human is to experience conflict so a supervisor has to know how to deal with it.

Prompt action is necessary otherwise the situation can escalate and more people become involved.

Set up a meeting at a mutually suitable time. It may be best to hold this on neutral ground and it must be free from interruption.

A logical sequence should then follow

(a) Respect the other person. The issue is about a situation, something that has happened. The people involved haven't changed but actions may have changed things. Keep the people and the situation separate.

(b) The emotional aspects of the conflict must be dealt with first. The attitude of the other person may be 'I want to fight (or yell, or cry, or swear) — I don't want to listen to reason! I want you to know how I feel'. Respond with reflective listening which will enable you to appreciate what is happening here and this should do much to reduce the tension provided that you keep your own emotions firmly in check. Then ask the person to re-state what he or she sees as the problem and what caused it.

(c) From your perspective you will probably see it differently. Start by saying that you want to identify these differences so that you can both examine them. It is your turn to communicate your side

- avoid emotive words
- distinguish between facts and opinions
- disclose your own feelings.

(d) Discuss the differences

- try and define the problem in terms of needs not of solutions
- identify common ground
- establish the unshakable facts
- agree on a joint objective.

(e) Move into collaborative problem solving

- explore all possible options
- select the best option which will best meet the needs of both parties. (First check the likely consequences)
- agree who will do what, where, how and by when
- follow up to ensure that what should have happened met your agreed objective.

If two groups are involved in a conflict situation another approach has led to satisfactory solutions

- bring the parties together, then
- each prepares a list for the other which shows what they would like to see the other
  continue to do
  start to do
  stop doing

if expectations are to be met and positive results achieved

- exchange lists and discuss
- the parties merge, discuss areas of agreement and negotiate on a resolution of the residual differences.

It would be useful to put the resultant agreement in writing.


## ABSENTEEISM

105

Absenteeism is a serious problem when it is intentional, without a valid reason, frequent. It will affect productivity, customer service and the performance and image of the work unit, and thereby your own leadership.

Absenteeism can have many causes — work-related situations, health or medical conditions, alcohol/drug problems, or other personal problems. Diagnosis of cause must precede any action and it may take very tactful discussion to identify the real reasons (and there may be several). Early attention is critical — absenteeism should not be allowed to continue.

You should stress the value and contribution of each person to the unit. The strongest preventer of absenteeism can be the cohesiveness and commitment of the work team, which is dependent upon individual effort. But if the situation continues and your counselling and other corrective actions have not resolved the issue disciplinary action may be the only solution.


## MAINTAINING DISCIPLINE

Perhaps this should be headed 'How to correct employees', for you should always aim for improvement, not punishment. There are two ways to discipline

- The positive way
  which prompts and encourages people to conform
  uses constructive help

develops correct working habits
enables a person to make corrections without losing face.
- The negative way
which uses threats and authority to get results
uses penalties and punishments or fear of them.

People want to know and have the right to know where they stand and to be quite clear what the rules are. This is the only condition in which discipline will be accepted. Each rule has to be seen to be appropriate and fair.

The 'hot stove' rule is a good guide here. When you touch a hot stove (marked 'don't touch') the discipline is immediate, with warning, consistent and impersonal. Anger or other emotion does not help because

- you had warning — you knew what would happen if you touched it
- the penalty is consistent — everyone gets the same treatment
- the penalty is impersonal — a person is burned not because of who he or she is, but because the stove was touched
- the penalty is not delayed.

The discipline should be concerned with the act, not with the person. This is important.

But this is a sensitive area, and you should be guided by your manager (and your employee relations officer, if appropriate) so that you are quite sure

- what authority you have to discipline
- what your contact with the shop steward or the union delegate should be in a disciplinary matter
- what actions you should take when confronted with a problem of discipline.

As a minimum you should
(a)  get **all** the facts and check them
(b)  seek to find the real reasons why the incident occurred
(c)  ensure that the rule was properly understood
(d)  know what actions should be taken when the facts are proven.
The formal procedure may be

- first offence — an oral warning, a spoken reprimand, given in the presence of a witness, recorded and then reported to your manager
- second offence — a written warning to follow an interview. This should include
  — a statement of the problem
  — identification of the rule which has been breached
  — the consequences of any further breaches
  — the employee's commitment, if any, to take corrective action
  — follow-up action to be taken, if any.

Your copy should be initialled by the individual as a form of receipt, and a copy may also be given to the union representative

— experience advises that if appropriate the union representative should be informed as soon as it has been decided to initiate formal disciplinary procedures. Often he or she can work with the supervisor to help resolve the issue. Should termination then be the outcome the union will already be fully aware of all the circumstances and there is unlikely to be any claim of wrongful dismissal

• third offence — this can be final action such as dismissal in terms of the award provisions.

This formal process should not be used until other ways of resolving the situation have been tried.

You must be very clear regarding your specific responsibility here. You may be able to give an oral warning, but can you give a written warning? Check with your manager.

*Note:* In formal disciplinary procedures all steps must be fully and accurately documented and the established procedures must be followed scrupulously. Any deviations could nullify your action.

Dismissal should be a last resort action. The primary purpose is to change behaviour without loss of dignity. The check list on page 108 should be studied carefully — and you should remember the point which is made under Problem Solving: 'Quick decision — long repentance'.

As with grievances, prompt action is necessary, but it must be the correct action. And it must be followed up to make certain that the matter has been satisfactorily resolved. But don't act impulsively. Think of all the possible alternatives and the consequences of what you are planning to do. Your aim is correction, and this in itself is a form of training.

People will inevitably 'try on' the new supervisor in a variety of ways to find out what his or her standards are. They need the assurance of knowing what is now acceptable and what is not. They also want to see how you react. Be aware of this and recognise the actions for what they are. Keep cool.

Keep a sense of perspective but start with the standards you expect to maintain. 'Whatever you accept you approve' is particularly relevant here.

'A good supervisor is one who can criticise your mistakes without making you feel like one of them.'

**A disciplinary check list**
1  *Was the employee aware of the rule he or she was dismissed for breaking?*
   (a)  is it stated in clear, simple language?
   (b)  what steps were taken to make the employee aware of it?
   (c)  how long has the rule been in effect?
2  *Is the rule reasonable?*
   (a)  is it acceptable as normal social and industrial practice?
   (b)  can it be applied consistently to all employees?
   (c)  is it justified for safety or economic reasons?
3  *Has the rule been enforced consistently?*
   (a)  is there any evidence that the employee has been 'singled out'?
   (b)  where appropriate, did the employees get the same training as other employees?
   (c)  have other employees broken the rule without being punished?
4  *Was the employee warned?*
   (a)  what corrective action was taken before dismissal?
   (b)  is there any evidence of a formal warning?
   (c)  was this warning challenged?
   (d)  has the company consistently dismissed employees after a 'final' warning?
5  *Was the company's decision based on facts?*
   (a)  what is the employee's past record?
   (b)  is dismissal a reasonable punishment in the light of this record?
   (c)  what has been the company's past practice where this rule has been broken?
   (d)  what actual damage did the company suffer?
   (e)  what damage could the company suffer if the rule continued to be broken?
   (f)  does the company have facts and figures to support its case?
6  *Does the industrial agreement cover the situation?*
   (a)  is it a term of the negotiated agreement?
   (b)  is it a commitment made by an authorised representative of the employer?

# CONTINGENT EMPLOYEES (NOT FULL-TIME)

The composition of the work force is changing. An increasing amount of work is now being done on contract or by temporary or part-time employees, and the impact of this on society has yet to be assessed.

It will certainly place a heavier responsibility on supervisors. People on contract are governed by the terms and conditions of their contracts and the quantity and quality of their output must meet agreed standards, but temporary employees are not subject to such control. A temporary employee has no tenure of employment and is primarily concerned with money received for work done and with resolving the uncertainty of the next job. Mission statements and exhortations for customer focus and quality output in a team environment will raise little enthusiasm or motivation.

Yet you, as their supervisor, are accountable for maintaining task outputs which meet set standards of quantity, quality, cost and time — and this will be done only by people committed to target achievement. Ways must be found of generating this commitment. Some of these might be

(a) By ensuring that each temporary employee knows and understands the purpose of the job and the standards required, and by the regular supply of information relating to it, including progress reports on results to date.

(b) By recognising that each person gets satisfaction from a job well done and from being part of a successful team — again this requires encouragement and communication from the supervisor.

(c) By challenging the group to tackle difficult but genuine tasks which have tight achievable targets requiring concentrated effort, and by rewarding success in an appropriate manner.

People really respond to challenge but few organisations seem to realise this.

(d) By accepting the limited duration of the employment and by seeking to give each person a measure of skill or knowledge which might enhance future work prospects. This can be done by negotiation at time of appointment on the basis of 'We'll train you in (nominated skill or knowledge) if you'll undertake to give us good sustained effort', and by encouraging each person to compile and maintain a **Work Experience Log Book** to record a personal statement of skill and knowledge acquired.

109

Sample pages of such a Log Book follow and it will be seen that every employee could benefit by keeping such a record.

## WORKING WITH PEOPLE OF OTHER CULTURES

Your work force may include people of several nationalities, and for some English will be their second language. Problems may then arise from two sources

### 1 Difficulties with language

English can be confusing — for instance, how many meanings can you give to the word 'fine' or to 'set'? And 'cleave' can mean to 'slice apart' or to 'cling to'. But it's worse than that. We all use a lot of jargon and slang in our everyday speech and every organisation has its own technical language of terms and abbreviations which seem to make sense only to those who work there. Should you have a 'glossary of terms used here' for your appointees? Test it.

If you ask 'did you understand that?' the answer will often be 'yes', which does not necessarily mean that your message has been understood. It may be a way of showing courtesy or of wishing not to become involved. If you ask, 'aren't you feeling well?' the answer 'yes' may mean from a person of another culture 'yes, I am not feeling well', but we usually interpret it to mean the opposite.

Use simple words and short sentences. Be patient. Get the person to repeat the message back to you in their own words, and be sure even then that he or she knows what the words mean. Use illustrations, the written word, and if necessary, an interpreter.

Printed instructions or notices may need to be multilingual. You may obtain considerable value in using multilingual Work Sheets or breakdown guides in teaching work skill.

You will gain much if you learn to say at least 'Good morning' and 'Thank you' in the language of your employees.

## 2 Cultural differences

These will vary with countries of origin, but you should try to understand differences which can affect work or human relationships. For instance, extended family ties may seem to be more important then attendance at work, hours of work may sometimes conflict with cultural obligations, and there could be many other problem areas.

If there is a large group of people from one race or nationality one of them can be used as a contact person or as an intermediary. This can be most helpful.

In one instance where the work force was of one racial group no one would apply for the supervisor's vacant position because to do so would be seen as an attempted assertion that the applicant felt superior to the rest of the group. But when they were asked to select the person they considered would be the best supervisor they responded thoughtfully and with obvious pleasure.

The important thing is you treat each person as an individual who has his or her own cultural heritage and dignity, and that to each you show respect, warmth, patience and understanding.

## WORKING WITH THE DISADVANTAGED

Every person is special — a mix of strengths and weaknesses, a person with needs, feelings and attitudes.

If a disadvantaged person is appointed to your group it will be because he or she has a special contribution to make to it and it is your responsibility to ensure that this happens and that they know it.

You should first ascertain what special needs they have; for instance, the work station may need some modification. Then you train to ensure that knowledge and skill will be fully used.

After that, and with due regard to the law of the situation, you give the employee no special treatment and deal with him or her as you do with the other valued members of your group. They are all members of your team.

**WORK EXPERIENCE LOG BOOK**

NAME:
ADDRESS:

PHONE:

### Introduction

We gain work experience in a variety of ways ranging from after-school or vacation jobs to part-time or temporary positions, or in full-time employment. But if we are seeking another job, perhaps in a new field, it is often very difficult to assemble in one spot just how much work experience and skill we really have accumulated. At an interview we may not be able to present ourselves to our own best advantage because we cannot produce this information.

This **Log Book** now enables you to build up a record of your work experience — what you have done to date and a more detailed record of your jobs from this time forward.

SCHOOL LEVEL REACHED:

MY BEST SUBJECTS:

I LEFT FORMAL SCHOOLING IN:

| QUALIFICATIONS GAINED SINCE THEN: | Dates |
| --- | --- |

COURSES ATTENDED:

| Title | Length | Dates |
| --- | --- | --- |

## Summary of work experience

This can cover either all your experience to date or be confined to the field in which you now wish to specialise.
**Skills gained** should show the actual skill, e.g. 'Receptionist/Switchboard', 'Operated 1-tonne forklift', 'Shop assistant — deli'.
**Nature of work** should show the type of business, e.g. 'City restaurant', 'Local Government — Mechanical Branch', 'Supermarket'

| Skill Gained | Nature of Work | Employer (or Voluntary Work) | Period |
|---|---|---|---|
| | | | |

## Work experience log

This will record the skills learned and used in each job you have done. A separate page should be completed for each employer. Ensure that this is completed before you leave that job.

NAME:

EMPLOYED BY:

FROM:

TO:

WORK SKILLS LEARNED AND PRACTISED: (and period spent on each)

ASSESSMENT OF COMPETENCY:

Rated by:
Position held:

**Learning contract**

You are responsible for your own growth. If you feel there are particular skills you need to make you more effective and it is in your power to do something about it a Learning Contract will challenge you to take action and to make a commitment. By making a contract with someone else, perhaps a friend, to achieve something by a specific date the effort will be reinforced.

*SKILL SOUGHT:*

*WHAT I PLAN TO DO:*

*TARGET DATE:*
*THIS WILL ACHIEVE:*

*I AM MAKING THIS CONTRACT WITH:*                    *ON:*

*I THEN PLAN TO DEVELOP MY SKILLS FURTHER BY:*

*SIGNED BY:*                    *ON:*

*My report on what was actually accomplished:*

116

# CHAPTER 7

# MAKING DECISIONS AND SOLVING PROBLEMS

## DECISIONS AND PROBLEMS

Every supervisory and front line manager is expected to be competent in solving the many problems which surface in every job every day.

And now when increasing attention is being directed to developing the abilities of the work force through team building processes problem solving is being delegated to the people involved — and the supervisor has to pass on the appropriate skills.

A decision is a choice between options and is a component of problem solving. A decision is also the action a manager or supervisor must take when the information is so incomplete that the answer does not suggest itself.

A problem is a deviation from what ought to be.

You and your team should constantly be looking for problems. Be pro-active and not just reactive. Your capacity to solve problems is a state of mind.

**Where there is no problem there can be no improvement**

Problem solving is one of the key tasks of every supervisor and it probably takes more time than anything else.

The traditional approach to optimal decision making is by six steps

1 **Identify your objective** (any problem will have an objective and one or more obstacles) — short and long term
2 **Define the problem**
    what are the indicators that this is a problem?
    who or what is affected by it now?
    what kind of problem is it?
    what is the critical factor?
    why does it have to be solved?
    when does it have to be solved?
    what will solving it cost?
    who should solve it?
3 **Think it through**
    what is likely to happen when it is solved?
    who will be affected?
    are you being influenced by your own feelings about the situation?
    what other external factors should you take into account here?
    what are the most important criteria for the solution?
    is this problem linked to other situations?
4 **Consider the alternative solutions**
    what are the possible options?
    list as many as you can
    what are the likely end results of each of these?
    which of them seems to be the best from all angles?
    does it meet all the criteria and the objectives?
5 **Take action**
    how and when?

can targets and target dates be set?
what resources are needed?
who must be informed? when? how?

6 **Follow–up**
what really happened?
now what?

(Under other circumstances, such as budgeting, incremental decision making may be more appropriate — what was done last time will be the basis for deciding what to do next.)

The sequence of action outlined above is logical but many other factors must be considered. Don't depend solely on facts. Decisions must be based on assumptions and there are no decisions without risks. By thinking carefully you can reduce the odds of doing the wrong thing. Don't be stampeded into hasty action. Don't jump to conclusions. Take time to consider all the possibilities, and then move confidently. Recognise that the inevitable will always happen.

Many things can and do influence your decisions and you should consciously be aware of these.

Two maxims are important:

### Quick decision — long repentance

(Sometimes expressed as — Don't test the depth of the river with both feet.)

For we do tend to push people into quick action. For instance, we've all heard 'Don't just stand there — do something!'

### Your decision is only as good as the best option you have considered

The common difficulty is that we tend to stay on the known paths and seldom seek to test the limits of the possible. It requires mind stretching to find all the options. There are other difficulties here.

One is a mental attitude rather than the spoken word. The likely outcome is 'I have made up my mind. Don't confuse me with any more facts'.

Another is to look for evidence which will support what you want to do and to brush aside factors which counsel otherwise.

Yet another can occur when a group is involved in the decision-making process.

The group can become so concerned with the problem itself that they do not notice what is happening in the group. Almost anyone with a strong voice and a confident manner can sway the group in the direction of his or her thinking to the point where the discussion becomes limited within the parameters of that approach — particularly so if that person is backed by one or two others. This can happen quite early in the meeting and unless the leader is alert to this it can be difficult to introduce other ideas or concepts radically different from what has been presented.

**Many things can influence your decision**

But there is a further element here. A decision has two ingredients
1   The quality and the wisdom of the decision
2   Its acceptance and implementation by those who will be affected by it and who can influence its effectiveness.

Suppose that in solving a particular problem there were four possible options — A, B, C and D — in that sequence, which meant that Solution A would be nominated. But if from discussion with those dealing with the problem it emerged that the preferred sequence was D, B, C and A, then it seems likely that the best results might be achieved by adopting option B.

This requires analysing problems to determine which objective is more important and then in planning action for optimum success — a balancing of the quality and acceptance factors.

In some instances involving the work group in the decision process may produce the best result, for example, who should get the new replacement machine?

Problem solving requires uninhibited creative thinking, but all too often the organisational environment and its culture create their own inhibitions. There are the obvious barriers, such as

— the one acceptable answer
— the self-imposed limitations
— the pressure to conform
— failing to challenge the obvious
— responding to short-term quick fix needs
— fear of doing the wrong thing.

And of these the pressure to conform, to hold the status quo, can be the most vocal. For instance, we've all probably heard some of these.

'It costs too much.'
'It can't be done.'
'It's too big a change.'
'We don't have the time.'
'We're too small.'
'Let's get back to reality.'
'It's not in the budget.'
Let's form a committee.'
'We already have too much to worry about.'
'So what else is new?'
'Let's check on it later.'
'What are you? Some kind of nut.'
'The boss will laugh.'
'It's great — but ....'
'Why not start today?'
'We tried that 25 years ago.'
'I thought of that last year, we didn't use it then.'
'Who needs it?'
'That's against all of our combined logic.'
'The public will laugh at us.'
'We've got enough problems already.'
'The upstairs won't like it.'
'The public is not ready yet.'

'You're on the wrong track.'
'Not enough return on investment.'
'Let's shelve that idea for a while.'
'Who is going to do it?'
'What do you know about it.'
'I don't understand what you hope to accomplish.'
'How does that concern you?'
'Someone must have done it.'
'I can't sell it.'
'Someday there may be a need for this.'
'Why do that now?'
'It's too risky.'
'Competition has taken the lead.'
'We tried that two years ago.'
'What for?'
'You'll never get approval.'
'You've got to be kidding.'
'Be sensible.'
'It's not a new concept.'
'It's probably illegal.'
'Why?'
'It won't hold water.'
'It won't fit our operation.'
'We're too big for that.'
'Don't be ridiculous.'

121

So supervisors have to take wider views of their objectives, to be aware of differing opinions and the reasons behind them, to be able to identify the common ground and to negotiate ways of achieving logical and cost-effective outcomes.

## IDENTIFYING THE PROBLEM

If something goes wrong it is because something has changed. That something must be identified.

A difficulty, of course, is that there are few single problems. Usually, they appear in diverse clusters, each demanding a measure of urgency. Some will be work based, others will be people based.

You have to prioritise. You have to make decisions. You have to manage your time (and Chapter 3 discusses this).

The first step is to identify the problem — the real problem, not the symptoms of it. This means analysing the factors which have produced it, separating facts from opinions, and seeking information, not scapegoats.

It has been suggested that if you ask 'Why?' five times the real problem will become clear, for instance

- Why did the machine stop?
  there was an overload
- Why was there an overload?
  the bearings weren't properly lubricated
- Why not?
  the lubricating pump wasn't working
- Why wasn't it?
  the pump shaft was worn
- Why was it worn?
  metal dust got inside because there was no protection around the shaft.

Then one needs to ask questions such as
Is this my problem? Can I delegate?
What is the worst case scenario in this situation?
In the light of my other tasks what priority does this demand? Is there a deadline?
Are there cost benefit elements in this?

But you should also be endeavouring to prevent problems arising. Think about all the aspects of your job and ask yourself 'What would happen if . . . .' Then take the appropriate corrective action.

## A RANGE OF TECHNIQUES

There are many techniques to assist in diagnosing the situation or in finding solutions, and some of these are described. You should try each when circumstances permit so that you become familiar with their potential. Your objective is to build an appropriate logic into your decision-making processes and to be able to select the best approach.

## (a) Decision Grid

This is a method of matching criteria with options and it can be used in a variety of ways from purchasing an item of equipment to staff selection.

Because some criteria are more important than others they can be weighted, say by the spread allocation of 100 points:

| Criteria | Weighting 100 | | | | Options | | | Notes |
|---|---|---|---|---|---|---|---|---|
| | | | | | | | | |
| | | | | | | | | |
| | | | | | | | | |
| | | | | | | | | |
| | | | | | | | | |
| | | | | | | | | |

123

A grid can be used to diagnose causes:

| Problem: | | | | | |
|---|---|---|---|---|---|
| | Lack of skill/ knowledge | A practical impediment | Lack of motivation | Inadequate instructions | |
| Output Quality Equipment Procedures People Impact | | | | | |

In another instance where too much rice was being grown and farmers were told to diversify their crops the farmers came together and with help from advisory staff compiled the following grid, worked through it as it related to their own farms and were enabled to make decisions based on logic and reasoned information rather than on emotion.

| Options | | | | | | | | | | |
|---|---|---|---|---|---|---|---|---|---|---|
| Key factors | Rice | Chili | Vegetables | Cowpea | Greengram | Soya bean | Groundnuts | Maize | | |
| Water | | | | | | | | | | |
| Income | | | | | | | | | | |
| Duration of crop | | | | | | | | | | |
| Marketing | | | | | | | | | | |
| Cultivation costs | | | | | | | | | | |
| Labour | | | | | | | | | | |
| Soil capacity | | | | | | | | | | |
| Seed availability | | | | | | | | | | |
| Drainage | | | | | | | | | | |
| Pest control | | | | | | | | | | |

## (b) Decision Tree

124

There will be occasions when the outcomes of consequences or options need to be set out so that the implications may be studied. A Decision Tree is one way of doing this and it also has significant value as a planning technique.

At each decision point the options are identified and expanded further. This technique ensures that options are fully explored and that the resultant decision has pre-knowledge of the likely consequences.

In the case of a project which is running behind schedule:

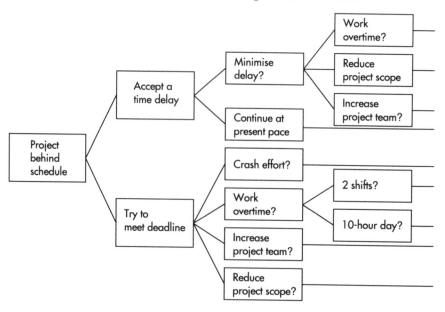

## (c) Force Field Analysis

This is a technique for studying a situation that you want to change. It requires the identification of the positive factors — the driving forces that indicate why action should be taken — and matching them with the negative factors — the restraining forces.

One approach is then to design action to strengthen the positive factors and to eliminate or reduce the negative factors.

| Situation: | |
|---|---|
| Driving forces — For | Restraining forces — Against |
| 1<br>2<br>3<br>4 | |
| Action plan: | |

125

Another proven use for this technique is when a personal major issue has to be decided — perhaps to change jobs, to relocate, to sell the house. This requires a second person (the observer) who is familiar with all the facts and the background of the situation who acts as your silent 'conscience', and two chairs representing the positive factors and the negative factors.

∩ observer

for ⊂ (< —— >) ⊃ against

First you discuss the issue from all aspects, then with the observer silent you sit in the 'positive chair' and tell the empty chair all the reasons why you should act, bringing out every bit of evidence (fact and feeling) you can muster. Then, perhaps after further discussion with the observer, you move to the 'negative' chair and tell the empty chair every reason why you should not take that particular stance. It has been found that this vocalising tends to bring out points which otherwise might stay concealed and a good result is usually achieved. (In one recent instance a husband and wife resolved to their mutual satisfaction a decision whether or not to emigrate.)

## (d) Brainstorming

Brainstorming is the unrestrained generation of ideas from a group directed towards a particular issue, or how to find solutions quickly, cheaply and effectively.

### Technique
1  Present the problem
(a)  this will usually be presented in negative terms. Get the group to re-present it positively by asking 'How to ......?' Several versions will emerge. Select the one which appears to offer the most promise and write it up.
2  Seek oral responses (brainstorm), with full participation
(a)  recorded on whiteboard or newsprint
(b)  allow no comment or criticism for this will dry up the flow of ideas
(c)  go for quantity of ideas at this point
(d)  encourage creative thinking without any limitation
(e)  suggest combining or modifying ideas already recorded
3  Evaluate ideas recorded, e.g.
(a)  important and feasible
(b)  possible
(c)  unlikely
      or another alternative might be as follows:

|  | Cheap to develop | Expensive to develop |
|---|---|---|
| High potential | A | B |
| Low potential | C | D |

4  Group to discuss and select the best which will most closely meet the criteria
5  Prepare and implement an action plan.

This participative approach encourages radical thinking and explores the limits of the possible. The leader must impose no restrictions.

Two other techniques, refinements of brainstorming, have evolved to meet particular needs and are widely used.

**The Delphi Technique** aims to obtain individual expert opinion from several sources on a particular problem, and then to obtain consensus and the best solution through a process of analysis, feedback, interaction and re-evaluation. There are variations to the approach but the common practice is as follows

- Each person records anonymously his/her preferred response
- These are then collated and analysed and a list is returned
- Each individual reviews the list and again records a preferred response
- A second collation and analysis is made
- The summary is then discussed fully by the group, a priority listing is made of the responses and through consensus the best solution is sought.

This technique minimises communication barriers such as hidden agendas and personality conflicts and focuses attention on the issue.

**The Nominal Group Technique** has similar features. The objective here is to generate a supportive progressive group committed to reaching a solution. In this

127

- Each person silently considers the issue, brainstorms the options and records his/her proposals
- These ideas are then written up in round-robin fashion (one response per person each time)
- Each person next evaluates these collective ideas and awards 5 points for the best, 4 for the next, etc.
- The votes are then tabulated. The best proposals are discussed and the optimum solution identified.

## (e) Mind Mapping

This is a form of brainstorming on paper. It recognises that whereas people have been educated into a pattern of linear thinking — making lists — in reality the mind darts all over the place, and in the time spent seeking to assemble material into lists good ideas can be lost.

An example of a mind map — 'Best Practice' — appears in the Preface to this book. Another is given earlier in this chapter — 'Many things can influence your decisions'. To start, identify, perhaps in the middle of a whiteboard, the problem and then build on the ideas that emerge. Extend each, exploring the thoughts that the heading generates, and link with dotted lines the interrelationships. For example, if your operating costs are too high:

'Just in time' ordering    Fewer lines    Improve work flow    Better maintenance

Reduce inventory    Reduce down time —— Multi-skilling of staff

Costs are too high

Reduce wastage by 60 per cent

Relocate    Reduce staff

Lower rents    Redundancy costs could offset savings    Best people will leave

Could improve work flow    Staff could leave    Loss of expertise

? Market image

This is clearly incomplete; you might like to build your own mind map from it, drawing on your knowledge of your own organisation.

## (f) Cause and Effect Analysis

Again this should be a participatory process which can include brainstorming to build up the 'fishbone' diagram.

'Effect' here is the outcome which is due usually to one of four causes

— people
— procedure
— equipment
— other.

The process is designed to identify and diagnose the factors which either singly or in combination create the problem.

In the example on page 129 the problem is poor quality reports to management.

Small working teams can be set up to do the analyses, to prioritise the problem areas, and to recommend or to put in place action targeted to remedy the deficiencies revealed.

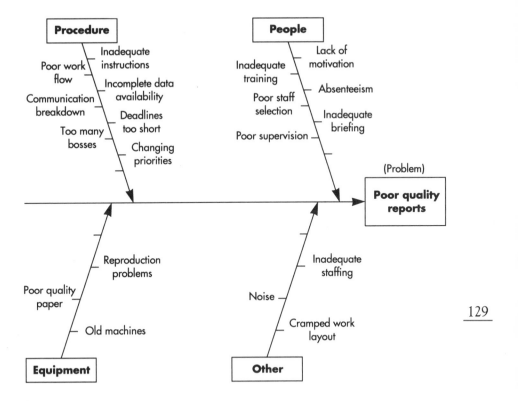

## (g) Making Good Decisions Quickly

Much of the work of supervisors requires good decisions, fast, and reputations can be made or broken on the success of the outcomes.

The seven-step sequence on the following page has been tested in a wide variety of situations and has proved to be most effective. While you are learning to use it the action sheet should be completed, but with practice it quickly becomes a mental drill (in this sequence) of
— situation
— objective
— facts
— real problem
— options
— solution
— action
but no step can be omitted.

A higher proportion of time spent in problem solving concentrates on symptoms not on causes. Whilst developing this particular procedure it was found in over 80 per cent of cases that during the examination of relevant facts the problem which had been presented changed and the underlying cause emerged.

## Problem Solving

1 **What appears to be the problem?**

2 **What is the objective (short and long term)?**

3 **What facts must be considered?**
   (Facts not opinions. Search for **all** relevant facts. To get beyond symptoms towards causes ask 'Why?' five times. Consider people, procedures, and other contributory factors.)

4 **What has now emerged as the real problem?**

5 **What options are or could be available?**
   (Explore widely beyond the obvious two or three. Brainstorming will help. Consider the advantages and disadvantages of each, including cost and time elements. Test by asking 'What if . . . ?' Will new problems be created?)

6 **The best option is**

7 **Action Plan**

In some cases the use of the following chart can be helpful in diagnosing the causes of the problem:

| The problem: | | |
|---|---|---|
| | *It is* | *It is not* |
| What is:<br>    the subject?<br>    the deviation? | | |
| Where in:<br>    the sequence?<br>    location? | | |
| When in:<br>    time?<br>    dates? | | |
| Extent:<br>    how many?<br>    how much?<br>    how often? | | |
| Pattern of deviations:<br>    trend?<br>    frequency? | | |
| Probable causes: | | |

> **After much time and effort**
> **coming up with good solutions to assumed problems**
> **while the deeper issues are not even identified**
> **is a major source of inefficiency**

Key points are

- The objective should separate the absolute requirements from the desirable factors
- Identify every relevant fact, not just a few
    test each by asking 'so what?'
    and if it doesn't matter it can be ignored
- Explore all possible options, go beyond the obvious.

### (h) Selecting the Best Option

Having generated options through some of the techniques described how do you then select the best?

There are several options

(i)   By using a grid, defining the specific criteria which the solution must meet and matching each option with them:

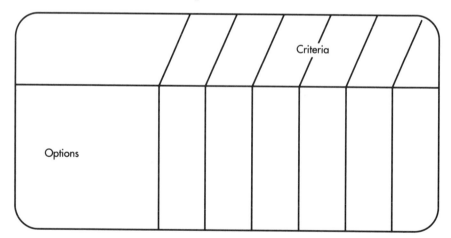

(ii)  By recording a 'yes' or 'no' or by using a scale e.g.

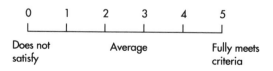

(iii) Compare the options with each other
e.g. If Option 4 is better than Option 2 record 4.

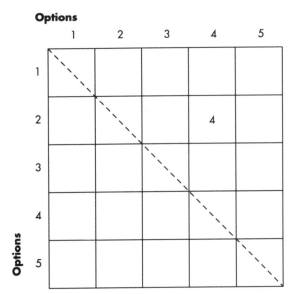

(iv) Forecast the possible consequences if each option were to be adopted, considering what could go wrong and assessing the likelihood of it happening and the effect of its impact.

**Option:**

| What could happen | Likelihood of happening (a) | Seriousness if it happens (b) | Consequence (a) × (b) |
|---|---|---|---|
| | 5 4 3 2 1 | 5 4 3 2 1 | |
| | 5 4 3 2 1 | 5 4 3 2 1 | |
| | 5 4 3 2 1 | 5 4 3 2 1 | |
| | 5 4 3 2 1 | 5 4 3 2 1 | |

(v) The Delphi and Nominal group techniques, described earlier under brainstorming, are further examples.

(vi) But there will be occasions when you have to make a decision yet you do not have all the vital information — the decision must be made. There are three logical steps

   1  Decide for each option whether the worst case scenario could be tolerated

   2  Decide for each option whether the best possible result is likely and inviting enough to justify risking failure

   3  Choose the option which appears to offer the best ratio.

It's more effective than flipping a coin.

## TEAM PROBLEM SOLVING

With the realisation that work groups accomplish more when they operate as teams which take responsibility for their own performance it follows that they should be more involved in problem solving and decision making. One of your training responsibilities is to equip your team with the skills to do this.

This means more than just teaching techniques like those described here. It means recognising the power being given to the team and being aware of its impact on the behaviour of the team. The outcomes could include the following

- Discussion within the team will sort out individual differences and tend to focus on what is fair for all
- Goals set will probably be high and may need to be adjusted after trial
- If the team is not criticised or made to feel inadequate it will develop constructive self-direction and will be responsive to performance challenges. Pride becomes a motivator
- The team will share on an equitable basis the pleasant and the not so pleasant tasks
- Once confidence is established the team will take risks in exploring options and in seeking more radical solutions to problems
- As the team leader your role here increasingly becomes that of a facilitator and advisor.

You don't have to solve all the problems yourself. There is a lot of talent in the people in your work group. Often they are the closest to the problem and will have their own ideas about it so tap into this resource. You should train your team in basic problem-solving skills as described earlier

- identify the problem and the objective
- examine the relevant facts
- consider all possible options
- select the best.

Then when a problem emerges they should be encouraged to produce a recommendation for resolving it.

Brainstorming and the cause and effect analysis are particularly relevant.

Another method is to initiate a discussion which will lead into the sequence of action described below — **Productivity improvement**. You could use this as a team building skill or as a way of developing one of your subordinates to whom could be delegated the responsibility for leading the project. For instance, if you were to initiate a drive to reduce waste two or three small Productivity Improvement Teams could be set up with people selecting which aspect they would like to study.

---

**Productivity improvement**

Select one area of activity where you work and set up a project using these headings:

Opportunity: what do we need to change to improve things or to remedy an identified problem?

Objective: what is the target?

How will we know when we've achieved it?

Timing: by when?

Tactics: how?

By whom?

Review progress on?

Result obtained:

---

In some organisations the team approach to problem solving has been developed under the name of **Quality Circles**.

A Quality Circle comprises a group of employees, led by their supervisor, who meet regularly in working time, usually for an hour a week, to learn a range of problem-solving skills, to apply these to problems which occur in their area of activity and then to submit their solutions to management in a formal presentation. The objectives of QCs are

- to reduce errors and improve quality
- to build stronger work teams by increasing involvement and thereby motivation
- to encourage personal and leadership development
- to create a problem-solving capability in the group
- to generate a commitment to higher productivity.

The key criterion for QCs' success is the sustained commitment to and involvement in the QCs' objectives by senior management and their recognition of the team efforts. If this is not maintained the enthusiasm for QCs' activity will diminish.

'**Value Added Teams**' usually operate in a similar way.

Unfortunately QCs in many cases have been seen as a nostrum— management's enthusiasm of the month — and the momentum has died. Inadequate recognition of success achieved has been a contributing factor. The 'What's in it for me?' element cannot be ignored.

As team leader you should constantly be asking 'What can we do to improve things around here?', selecting targets and initiating appropriate action.

> If you don't find a solution does that make you part of the problem?

## SOLVING PEOPLE BASED PERFORMANCE PROBLEMS

This is probably one of the most important sections in the book, because inevitably you will at times need to discuss with an individual a problem relating to poor performance or to what you believe to be some error of omission or commission. Mastery of the four-step method described below will give an insight into dealing with most people problems.

Because you are responsible for the output of your group the performance of each person is important. But for a variety of reasons this performance may not always meet the required standards. At the first sign of this you must take action with the person concerned. And this calls for a special skill.

1  **You can deal with it or ignore it** and hope that the problem will resolve itself — usually it won't, it will get worse.

2  **Analyse the situation**

- Are there standards? Are they
    clearly defined?
    mutually acceptable?
    mutually understood?

    If standards are not clear how do you know they are not being met? Once they are agreed plans can be made for their achievement.

- Consider the personal and impersonal issues
    are you overreacting?
    how much of the fault is yours?
    what emotions are involved?
    what type of reaction are you seeking?
    what is the previous work record of this person?

- Plan the discussion
    is your objective quite clear? (do not proceed until it is)
    consider timing and place (neutral ground may be desirable).

137

3  **Have the discussion**
The key components are

- Empathy
    establish a wave-length which is factual and unemotional, communication which levels and which enhances or builds up self-esteem. Empathy responds to feelings

- Present the facts
    unadorned, free from opinions and hearsay. This should be the beginning of negotiation so separate the problem from the person.

If you attack or are thought to be attacking the individual there will be an immediate negative reaction and a withdrawal from any hoped for co-operation. At this point both parties will take a particular stance and neither will find it easy to back down.

> Anger gets us into trouble
> Pride keeps us there

- Action
    your purpose should be collaborative problem solving. Seek positive not negative responses. Listen. Encourage expression of feelings and of ideas for resolving the situation. Explore the options. Prepare an action plan.

### 4 Follow-up

how satisfied are both parties?
did you achieve a win-win or a win-lose solution?
what really was accomplished?
was the objective achieved?
now what?

You cannot avoid these situations. You are expected to deal with them competently.

The following sequence will help you in dealing with most people problems and it is suggested you copy it on to a card for quick reference (Do not omit any steps):

1 **Maintain the self-image of the individual**
2 **Establish the facts**
3 **Agree on objectives**
4 **Listen with empathy**
5 **Ask for ideas**
6 **Explore all options**
7 **Seek a win-win solution**
8 **Follow up**

The algorithm which follows on page 139 will also be helpful.

## When people are not performing effectively

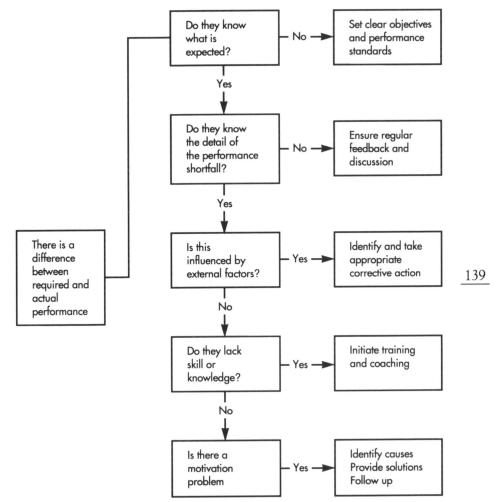

## ACTION — THE IMPLEMENTATION HURDLE

When you have solved the problem or made the decision the action is not yet complete. The final step is implementation.

You can probably recall an occasion when a good decision foundered because administrative people handled it clumsily.

The primary task is to create a climate in which implementation can take place smoothly. This will require

planning
communication
action
follow-up.

Each of the following questions must be considered, because a break-down here can nullify all your effort in problem solving

(a)  Purpose of implementation?
        what precisely is to be done?
        by whom? By when?
(b)  How will it be done? (Outlining this as part of the recommendation will often ensure its acceptance)
(c)  Who is responsible for action? For coordination?
(d)  Who will be affected?
        how?
(e)  What should they be told?
        when? By whom?
        what advance information can be released?
(f)  Have the benefits to be derived been identified? and, have the possible problems been identified?
(g)  What could prevent or slow down implementation?
(h)  Who or what could assist implementation?
(i)  Likely effect upon other functions or departments?

You ignore these questions at your peril.

> Can you identify a recent situation in which there seemed to be difficulty in securing effective implementation?
>     what went wrong? Why?
> Is another situation coming up?
>     what must be done to ensure success?

When the action will affect members of your own work group you should consider whether and to what extent you should confer with them in reaching your decision. On some occasions you must act alone. On others you might let them decide. For instance, if they all use identical machines and a new one is allocated to the group, who gets it? The decision must be seen by all to be fair. If the group decides, the issue will be resolved in terms of sets of values and needs existing in the group at that time. Everyone must be aware of each other's needs and by discussion they will realise that fairness cannot be achieved by judging others.

But here, as elsewhere, your action must be governed by the law of the situation.

There is one way both to improve yourself and to practise decision making. Next time you meet a problem you cannot solve immediately — the kind of problem you used to refer to your manager for action — try and analyse it using some of the steps described above. Then go to your manager and say 'The problem as I see it is .................... The options appear to be.

(1) .................... (2) .................... or (3) ...................., and of these I would recommend option (...), but I'd welcome your opinion'.

---

### A Check list

**Find** the problem — the cause of the concern
**Facts** — identify all relevant information
**Filter** — eliminate the unimportant
    Ask 'Why?' five times
**Focus** — on the real problem
**Ferret out** — all the possible options
    Consider the likely consequences of each
    Select the best
**Fix** — prepare an action plan
    Assign responsibility, authority and resources to do the job
**Follow up** — did the solution adequately meet the situation?
**Feedback** — were any new problems generated from this?
**Felicitate** — commend those involved in fixing it.

141

# CHAPTER 8

# HEALTH AND SAFETY AT THE WORK PLACE

The Supervisor's Obligations
Safety Inspections

## THE SUPERVISOR'S OBLIGATIONS

One of your continuing responsibilities is safety at the work place.

- Is this defined in your Job Description?
     if not, why not?
     what performance output is expected?
- Do you have annual records of accidents affecting your area of work over the last five years?
- Do you have similar records of accident costs? e.g. lost time of people or in work flow?
- How often does management discuss safety with you?
     is there an approved safety policy?
     are there established safety rules?

An accident is an unplanned event caused by an unsafe act or an unsafe condition. Your task is to identify and assess these hazards and to take action to remedy them as quickly as possible.

This will require

(a) **Your leadership and a sharing of responsibility**
— what you do carries more weight than what you say, so your personal example must be good at all times. You should do nothing or accept no condition which is or could become a hazard or a risk
— responsibility for safe working conditions or precautions should be shared with members of the unit but you should police everything. **That which is not inspected will deteriorate**, but you should also encourage each member of your unit to become aware of the importance of safety and to try and make both the work and the work place free of hazards
— unions share your concern for health and safety and you should seek the active involvement of union representatives in identifying and correcting safety hazards.

(b) **Compliance with all relevant regulations**
— certain statutes require that specific safety precautions be taken — the Construction Act, Factories Act, Health and Safety in Employment Act, etc.
— find out from your manager precisely what your responsibilities are under the law, get them in writing if at all possible, and make certain that they are known and understood by each member of your unit. They may need to be displayed, and in any case they should be
— if you have a multi-cultural work force, for some of whom English may not be their everyday language, you should arrange translations of all displayed safety notices
— are there any factors in the work area or work environment which create or could create a health hazard?

(c) **The maintenance of safe working conditions**
— good housekeeping, the proper maintenance of plant, equipment and tools, the use of protective clothing and safe working habits are all essential. Many accidents happen in offices
— encourage people to look at the work place each day as though they had not seen it before and to look for possible hazards
— swap with another supervisor and do a hard-headed safety inspection of each other's unit
— this should also be a shared responsibility for employees have a legal duty to take care to protect their own health, safety and welfare and to avoid wilfully affecting the health and safety of any other person. They have a close knowledge of their own work place and, therefore, can make significant contributions on health and safety matters.

(d) **Safety training and emergency drills**
  — when teaching work skills, using work sheets, add a final column 'safety factors' to highlight action needed to avoid hazards
  — people need to know about machine guarding, eye protection, the handling of dangerous goods, lifting techniques, what to do in case of fire, flood or earthquake, etc. If you can't give this training yourself discuss with your management how best it may be obtained, but make sure it is given and repeated
  — set aside a specific time for this training
  — have practice drills
  (i) does the organisation have a major disaster plan showing who should do what and who are the back-up people? What is your role and that of your unit? Does everyone know this?
  (ii) who is authorised to speak to the media?

(e) **Availability of first aid and medical facilities**
  — in an accident bleeding, poisoning, heart or breathing arrest, and shock must be treated immediately; most other things can await the arrival of trained help. Could you cope?
  — do you know what first aid help you can call on? and how far away is it? Does your first aid box carry an updated list of trained people and show where they are working?
  — should you be given first aid training?

(f) **An efficient accident reporting system**
  — the law says you must keep an accident record, and from an interpretation of your records you may be helped to determine and correct the causes of accidents
  — most organisations have their own form of accident reports, but you should be able to record the answer to two questions
  (i) what really caused this accident?
  (ii) what do we need to do so that it cannot happen again?
  — your accident reports should, if possible, end with a corrective recommendation, which you should follow up.

Industrial accidents do not happen in a vacuum. They result from the actions of individuals, who are usually members of a group. Some individuals, or some groups, seem to have more accidents than others. Certain jobs are more hazardous. What do the statistics show in your organisation? You should know this.

All accidents are very costly. There are not only the direct medical and compensation costs, but also the indirect costs which could include
lost time by fellow employees
lost time by supervisors
damage to tools, equipment or plant

spoiled work
loss of production
costs of recruiting and training a new employee
other items.
It has been estimated that the indirect costs of any accident will be at least nine times as great as the direct costs.

And in terms of lost time and lost production a near accident can be just as costly.

One thing seems certain. You will have to take positive steps to convince your employees that accidents are caused and can happen at any time. Most people go through life believing that an accident is something which happens to somebody else.

## SAFETY INSPECTIONS

Working safely is habit forming, and rapidly develops into group pride in being part of an accident-free operation. It could be morale building to have a chart showing '. . . days without an accident here'. This is a measure of your leadership. Even if your organisation has a safety officer, you are responsible for the safety of your unit. He or she is there to assist you. You should be constantly seeking to detect unsafe actions by people or unsafe conditions which could cause accidents.

145

Imagine that you will be penalised by a monetary fine for every safety hazard found at your work place. How often would you be paying?

Crisis training is very relevant here.

You should make regular checks — but as part of your drive to make and keep your team safety conscious each of them should from time to time be given the responsibility of also making these checks.

This should be on the agenda of all staff meetings.

| Safety report by: | | Date: | |
|---|---|---|---|
| Unsafe conditions | Caused by | Action needed | Target date |
|  |  |  |  |
| Unsafe acts |  |  |  |
|  |  |  |  |

A simple procedure is

- examine each job and the work place
- identify hazards or possible hazards
- act to correct
- check back.

An in-built attitude to safety (and, of course, to other things) is developed from

learning and training + habit + feelings + feedback.

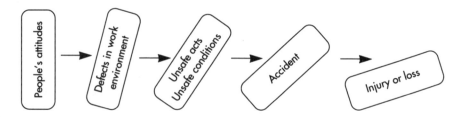

The domino effect leading to injury or loss

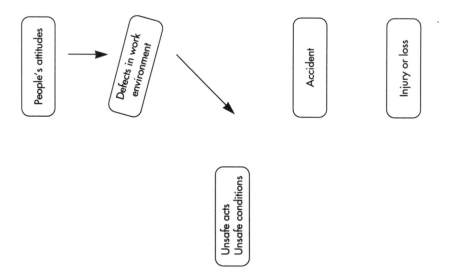

146

Remove 'unsafe acts' and 'unsafe conditions' and you remove the consequence of an accident, thus clearing the way to deal with the other causes of concern.

Your responsibility covers

- your employees
- the work methods
- the work area and its components.

**All must be safe.**

You have two further areas of responsibility

## Rehabilitation

An accident, or even a near accident, will have consequences for the individual. These may be physical, perhaps in the form of a disablement, or mental, which may be evidenced by a loss of confidence or a behavioural change. But as long as the individual is a member of your unit you have a duty of care.

The rehabilitation action needed can range from quiet discussion, to retraining, to modification of the work station, or to a change of duties, but it must be appropriate to the situation and be maintained as long as the need exists.

A major accident or incident may have wider effects affecting all or part of your unit and outside assistance may be needed to restore normality. Much will depend here on your leadership skills and upon the cohesiveness and mutual support of your unit team who will have to demonstrate appropriate adaptability. Special care may be needed in assigning priorities and in delegating tasks.

147

## Environmental

Your unit and your organisation operate in a wider environment within your community, and care of the environment in all its forms now demands a high priority which in many instances is reinforced by legislation. This is primarily an organisational responsibility but you should discuss with management the obligations which could devolve on your unit, and these should be shared with your employees.

# PART 3

**LEADING
YOUR TEAM**

# CHAPTER 9

# BUILDING AND DEVELOPING THE TEAM

## WHAT MAKES PEOPLE WORK WELL?

If the question were 'what makes people work?' the answer might be easier. For many the reason would be money, for some it would be social companionship, for others it might be personal ambition or an in-built work ethic.

But when you ask questions, such as

- 'What gives us an edge in the marketplace?'
- 'Do we have above average employees who are committed to the achievement of agreed objectives?'
- 'Are we appointing top-level people?'
- 'Do we have a problem with absenteeism?'

it becomes apparent that pay must be adequate and be felt to be fair if people are going to work for you but that other things will be necessary if they are to be willing to sustain better than average output in every respect.

> Under what conditions do you do your best work?

So, what will encourage them to put in extra effort, to take pride in work, so that objectives are achieved? The answers will vary but the common factors will usually include:

**doing something worthwhile — a goal**
'my work is interesting and varied. I'm part of a team. We understand why the work is important and the standards set are reasonable.'

**doing one's share — participation**
'others in my group depend on me. My ideas are listened to. The boss discusses things with us.'

152

**counting for something — recognition**
'they recognise me as a person and for what I can do. I get credit for good work, and help in trouble. I feel part of the group.'

**knowing what's going on — communication**
'I know how I'm doing, where I fit, what's going on, and why. Changes are discussed in advance with us and our ideas are sought.'

**getting a decent living — fair wages**
'my pay seems right for the skill, conditions, and importance of the job and for the effort I put out, and in relation to that of others.'

**preparing for the future — learning**
'I'm encouraged to develop new skills and to acquire new knowledge. I can see stepping stones along which I can advance.'

**doing things together — team work**
'we know the target. We know the score. We take pride in being a team that achieves results.'

Could your employees each say these things? If not, should you do something about it?

This is not an isolated problem. A notice in an Asian newspaper read:
*The Institute of Modern Management will hold a two day programme on "How to get work from people during working hours"....'*

Organisations are only as good as the people in them
People are only as good as the organisation enables them to be

But don't think you can motivate your people — you can't. Motivation is the internalised drive towards the dominant thought of the moment.

All you can do is to generate a situation to which people will respond because they want to. And this is your high priority.

As an individual you have personal objectives and only your own impediments can inhibit your achieving them.

But as a supervisor it is your people who will do the work which may or may not achieve the objective. They will have their own ideas about the organisation, about you, each other, outside factors, and the objective. The outcome to a degree is in their hands — your task is to get their interest and their commitment.

153

Each person brings to the job his or her own motivation and you should try to learn what this is. You should let it be known you expect the best from each and identify individual strengths so that you may build on to them. This will be infinitely more productive than pointing out weaknesses and expecting people to change. It should not be overlooked that **people tend to be what they are expected to be**.

Insecurity and uncertainty are the strongest demotivators

It could be interesting and valuable at one of your staff meetings to find out how your staff see their work and its environment. Ask them, working individually, to rate the factors listed in the 'in our work group' sheet, and then lead a constructive discussion to seek specific improvement.

## In our work group

(a) We have clear work objectives.

1 2 3 4 5 6

We're not clear about our objectives.

(b) Communication upward and downward is good. We always know what is going on. Our views are listened to.

1 2 3 4 5 6

No one tells us anything and we get most of our information from the grapevine.

(c) We usually work together very harmoniously.

1 2 3 4 5 6

There seems to be conflict too often and we're not very co-operative.

(d) We're keen to achieve results and take pride in performance.

1 2 3 4 5 6

It's just another job with people telling us what to do.

(e) The impact of change is discussed with us before it hits us.

1 2 3 4 5 6

We're told about change only after it's happened and we usually oppose it.

(f) Grievances are discussed fully and frankly and quick solutions are sought.

1 2 3 4 5 6

Grievances are not handled well. Things go underground and fester.

(g) We're given a job and encouraged to get on with it.

1 2 3 4 5 6

Someone is always breathing down our necks.

(h) The group seems to exercise its own standard of discipline.

1 2 3 4 5 6

People seem to look for things they can get away with.

(i) We look for better ways of doing things.

1 2 3 4 5 6

The pattern has been set so we stick with it.

(j) It feels good being part of this group.

1 2 3 4 5 6

There's nothing special about working here.

154

But do not use this or any other similar survey unless you are prepared to commit yourself to follow-up action. Issuing it generates an expectation that something will happen — and if nothing does your credibility will be damaged.

People will support what they have a part in. They will respond to challenge, goals towards which they can strive.

This is one of your responsibilities, for the success of your staff is your success.

> In one company a customer wanted a task done which management felt would have been too tight a deadline, but when asked the work force asserted they could do it — and by extra effort (and with no special incentive) they did it with time to spare. Then they said to management 'That was great. Why don't you give us more challenges like that?'

And in a survey of some 4000 wage workers in Australia some 60 per cent said they could improve production and reduce costs by at least 20 per cent if management sought their ideas — which up to that point it had not.

Two very evocative questions to ask are

- 'What is management doing that limits your ability to do your job?'
- 'What could management do that would make your job easier and yet improve productivity?'

155

But here too you can't walk away from what they tell you. You must follow up.

Therefore, if you want your unit to show pride in its work, to be highly productive, and to seek better methods of doing things, each person in it must feel that he or she has continuing

However, organisations — and supervisors — need to be aware of a very real mismatch between theory and reality for people tend to do the things they believe ought to be done.

A basic fact of life is that **the things that are rewarded get done** and you need to ask what gets rewarded where you work. For instance

— if management calls for high quality but sets extremely tight deadlines for completion

— if a manager has an autocratic obsession about housekeeping standards

— if management calls for creativity and innovation but represses mavericks and gives only lip service to new ideas and to a need for research

— if management seeks employee participation but makes unilateral decisions without consultation

— if management wants teamwork but stresses individual effort
what will actually be rewarded?

It is extraordinarily difficult to break down the barriers created by perceived double standards.

**Where you work what behaviours are rewarded?**
— is this what should be happening?

Perhaps clarity lies in the definition of the word 'participation':
— Supervisor A believes it is 'I tell my people what to do and they participate in doing it.'
— Supervisor B believes 'Management decides what has to be done and then I lead my team in a practical discussion on the best way to do it. We share ideas but I have to make the decisions.'

The best results and heightened morale are achieved when people get satisfying answers to basic questions, such as

- tell me what you expect of me
- tell me the standards by which my performance will be judged
- tell me how I'm getting on
- keep me informed about what is happening and about changes which will affect me
- teach me to develop new skills and to use them
- reward me according to my contribution
- provide stepping stones along which I may advance.

How often do you talk about these things with each of your people?

People respond to
work that has meaning
respect that is mutual
communication that levels
learning that is continuous.

In your own position consider

- How much responsibility is there in the jobs under your control?
  — each person should have a job or a parcel of jobs for which he or she is personally responsible
- To what extent is each a 'whole' job?
  — no one likes crumbs or bits and pieces
- What challenge does the job provide?
  — some variety seems most desirable
- How much opportunity is there to participate in problem solving and decision making?
  — people like to contribute
  — whose job is it anyway?
- How much feedback is provided about performance and other activities?
  — everyone wants to know what is happening
- How is performance — both of the group and of the individual — recognised?
  — most organisations have a lot of untapped talent

If you blame poor performance on your staff
who appointed them?
who trained them?
who coached them?
what motivates them?

## COACHING AND COUNSELLING

### Coaching

Coaching is the supportive technique used by the supervisor in giving guidance to subordinates, and is job-related.

It is generally accepted that some 90 per cent of all training is done on the job — often by copying what others do — and coaching should be an essential component of this. It is also recognised that a person's development is 90 per cent the result of his or her experience in the day-to-day work.

If you see yourself as the leader of a team of people working toward objectives then they will need your coaching, both individually and collectively. This is one of your personal responsibilities and somehow you will have to organise your day so that you will have time to do it.

Four steps are involved

- Observation of a personal or a group need
- Analysis of the circumstances which created this situation
- Diagnosis of the situation to determine the appropriate response or stimulus to meet the demonstrated need
- Helping the person or the group to recognise the problem and the solution, to accept ownership of it, to plan a course of action and to act to achieve a nominated target.

If the right climate has been created people will let you know when they need this help, and you should look for coaching opportunities to solve work problems and to develop personal skills and knowledge.

The primary requirement is your genuine wish to help others to help themselves. Coaching is a blend of asking, showing, telling, experimenting, a lot of listening, encouraging, and following up. It creates a learning situation. **Setting projects is a valuable technique.**

It takes a lot of practice to become a good coach and it requires a very positive attitude towards the organisation, the individual and the team tasks.

A guideline from the handbook of a sports coach suggests that a coach

- operates from the sidelines and listens, observes and analyses
- encourages learning by doing
- sets clear but high standards
- sets specific targets and deadlines and gives feedback
- works on one thing at a time
- asks questions to encourage thinking
- creates a climate of confidence
- allows for individual differences and strengths
- provides back-up support
- takes time, has patience and earns respect
- continues to coach.

But it is not necessarily a one person task. As the team develops people should begin to coach each other. The more experienced and competent coach the less capable and the whole group is constantly seeking ways of doing things more effectively.

## Counselling

Counselling is a process by which one person seeks to help another. Its objective is to generate self help. It is based on certain fundamental human needs

- the need to be dealt with as an individual rather than as a case or a category
- the need to express one's feelings, both positive and negative
- the need to be accepted as a person of worth and innate dignity, regardless of the person's dependence, weaknesses, faults or failures
- the need for an empathetic understanding of and response to the feelings expressed
- the need to be neither judged nor condemned for the present situation
- the need to make one's own choice and decisions concerning one's own life and not to be pushed around or manipulated
- the need to keep confidential the personal circumstances and feelings.

Clearly this requires the person doing the counselling to have special skills, which can be learned. It should not be undertaken without such skills. This role requires one to take a distinctly different stance from the usual supervisor/subordinate relationship and the chemistry of the human interaction has to be supportive and non-threatening. Listening, non-critically, nonjudgementally and reflectively, is a key skill. So too is the posing of evocative open-ended questions.

Counselling provides the opportunity to step back from the problems of the day and to focus with empathy on the needs of an individual. It can be appropriate to a special situation or it can be used to follow the appraisal interview.

The sequence of action will include

- setting aside adequate time for the meeting
- not prejudging the outcome
- agreeing on an objective
- creating a relaxed and helpful atmosphere free from interruption
- assisting the person to recognise and accept the real problem: separating fact from opinion and identifying all the facts
- seeking to clarify any hidden agenda items
- the identification of all possible options and the possible consequences of each
- assisting the person to select their best option and in formulating an action plan
- leaving the door open for further follow-up.

The objective is to assist the individual to

- gain insight into the real problem
- discuss it fully and rationally
- formulate constructive actions for resolving it
- accept ownership of the solution.

Counselling is best done on neutral ground away from the work place and free from time constraint.

## DEVELOPING PEOPLE FOR GROWTH AND PROMOTION

If each member of your unit is thought of as a member of the team, then each has an important part to play. But many supervisors underestimate the abilities and potential of some of their people, particularly younger new employees, whether they are unskilled or university graduates. Also, the capacities of older employees, those in the 40-plus age group, for re-training are often not recognised. These supervisors usually try to recruit specially the skilled employees they need, ignoring the untapped and undeveloped potential in the employees they already have. Their super-vision is seldom effective.

Goethe, the German writer, summed things up when he said: 'If you treat a man as he is, he will remain as he is. If you treat him as if he were what he could be and should be, he will become what he could be and should be.'

160

People tend to meet your expectations of performance if they know what they are, and they support them.

In developing your people there are several things you can do. You can rotate the jobs. You can enlarge the job. You can delegate. You can coach. The outcome is **multi-skilling**.

**Job rotation** means training people to do more than one job — this can be illustrated in a Capability Chart. You should not have to step in if someone is away, for while you have your coat off doing the work no one is running the unit. Other more important things may suffer.

No one should be moved to another position until fully competent in the present duties. Jobs vary in difficulty and people learn at different speeds so you should avoid a danger in changing everyone's jobs at regular intervals, but for each job you should have more than one trained person.

With the explosive growth of new technology the development of a multi-skilled work force is now becoming a necessity. Job rotation, backed by a well-structured training programme, is one approach to multi-skilling which should be included in organisational manpower planning.

**Job enlargement** means extending present duties by giving more responsibility either vertically or laterally. It is particularly useful when the line of advancement is within a narrow discipline, but it can be used in a variety of situations.

With organisations now having fewer levels in their hierarchical structures new promotional procedures will have to be devised. Vertical job enlargement offering each position more advancement steps is one logical solution.

**Delegation** means giving the employee the responsibility, the authority, and opportunity to handle the details of a job, and an obligation to report back. Delegation gives people the chance to respond to a challenge, to see what they can do. Allocate tasks so that each member of the unit is tested from time to time in a variety of situations (not all at once!) and encouraged to build up skills and confidence. If you do not do this you will never know what abilities waiting to be developed lie hidden in people.

You should not delegate matters relating to overall unit planning and control, to discipline, to staffing recommendations or to personal counselling and don't delegate things that can't be controlled, but beyond these you probably can entrust others with a measure of responsibility. For instance, **if a routine has been established for a particular task responsibility for it can usually be delegated**. One guideline here is that you should delegate to the most junior person capable of doing the job, and at the level at which all the facts are known.

A suggested method for delegating some of your tasks in which routines are already set is shown in the example 'Delegate — Now' (see page 162).

Remember, however, that when you delegate a job you remain accountable for whatever is done. Delegation is a matter of trust. Some people may make mistakes. Some may not do the job the way you would. Some will need more help than others. You role is to train these people, to encourage them to gain the confidence which comes with competence, and to provide back-up assistance when needed. Seek to use the capacity of young people when you are delegating, and you should remember the fact that older employees have an ability, often untapped, to be taught new skills. It takes courage to delegate, and this is a measure of your own confidence. You should set clear targets and get regular reports on progress.

161

If you can't develop talent within your unit, management may see you as the only person with all the skills and knowledge required. And if you are indispensable you can't be promoted.

If you are not delegating you are creating dependent people.

**How do you delegate?** One way is to encourage your people not to bring you problems but to bring you recommendations — and then perhaps to ask them 'what options did you consider?'

Delegate what you know, not what you don't know.

Another method is
1   List all the tasks done by the unit in order of importance, showing for each how much time it takes during a four-week period of 160 hours (see 'Delegate — Now').
2   Mark the tasks that you personally must do (and show why). Be careful not to include things just because you like doing them. Ask in each case 'Why must I personally do this?'

3 Work out a pattern that gives everyone in the unit over a period the chance of doing a range of tasks, and of being properly trained to do them.

4 Follow up and give special coaching where necessary.

**Delegate — Now**

**Then, estimate your time saving** (target: at least 1 hour per day)

| | (N) (T) | Members of your staff | | | | |
|---|---|---|---|---|---|---|
| | | Matthews | Thacker | Paige | Lewis | Leda |
| • List your regular tasks which take at least 10 minutes each | | | | | | |
| • Decide which you can assign now, and to whom and which you can assign after training | | | | | | |
| (a) Weekly statistics report | | | | | × (T) | |
| (b) Stock ordering | | × (N) | | | | |
| (c) Misc. personnel reports | | | Perhaps in 2 months | | | |
| (d) Analysis of performance printouts | | | | × First 2 stages (T) | | |

Delegation requires

| | | |
|---|---|---|
| reasons | : | what you wish to achieve |
| results | : | the outcome expected |
| assignment | : | of responsibility and authority and definition of limits |
| resources | : | what is available |
| deadlines | : | reporting and completion dates |
| feedback | : | on performance progress |
| control | : | what controls must be met |
| support | : | where to get help or training |

For successful delegation
    share the duties fairly — don't create a 'crown prince' who gets all the opportunity
    show appreciation for a job well done
    don't insist upon things being done your way
    keep people informed regarding policies, rules and precedents
    set attainable goals and deadlines
    help your staff to reach them
    coordinate their activities
    work for group success
Your own reputation depends on it.

163

Delegation is concerned not with allocating tasks but with giving results to achieve.

But you should also be training someone, or sharing tasks between a few, so they can take over your job if you are away. Management will expect the work to go on, and this is one way of preparing and testing people for promotion.

There is another side to this.
    Do you feel you could handle more delegated authority?
    If so why not ask for it?
    But be quite specific about what authority you want and why you want it.

The example 'Do you want more authority?' lets you make your own reasoned case for this — and if you can demonstrate how it will make your manager's job easier you'll probably get it.

Imagine that you are climbing steadily up a promotional ladder and that you'd like to reach up for the next rung or step. But you will be unable to move until you let go the one you're hanging on to. And if you don't delegate you can't let go. (Which means, of course, no more holidays either!)

**Do you want more authority?**

1. Do you feel you have sufficient authority now to meet the output requirements of your position?

   ☐ Yes     ☐ No

2. List below what further authority you believe should go with your position now.

| Job | Authority sought (define its limits) |
| --- | --- |
|  |  |
|  |  |
|  |  |
|  |  |
|  |  |

3. Who would be affected by this?

4. What would be the consequences?

5. Taking a helicopter view, what are the matching arguments for and against your case? Be realistic.

| For | Against |
| --- | --- |
|  |  |
|  |  |
|  |  |
|  |  |
|  |  |

6. So, what action will you take now?

164

# WORKING WITH A WINNING TEAM

A team has been defined as an energetic group of people who are committed to achieving agreed objectives, who work co-operatively together and enjoy doing so, and who produce high quality and effective results. The enthusiasm to generate the concept of team work in the work place has been driven by the need to improve quality and productivity to gain competitive advantage.

Few people work entirely on their own. Most are members of groups of one kind or another. And each of these groups should seek to develop the components of team work. The Chairman of the Board should be leading a team of fellow directors. The chief executive officer (CEO) should be leading a team of senior managers. Each senior manager should be leading a team of managers. Each manager should be leading a team of supervisors and each supervisor should be leading a team of employees.

That's the ideal — unfortunately it's not the reality for many organisations still see team work as a programme which somehow can be introduced at a middle or front line management level and which will quickly create higher profits or increased effectiveness. These organisations will be disappointed and the outcomes may well be the reverse of expectations.

Team work means giving responsibility, through training, trust and empowerment, to the people who do the work — and the people concerned have to want it.

The organisational concept of a team based structure is:

165

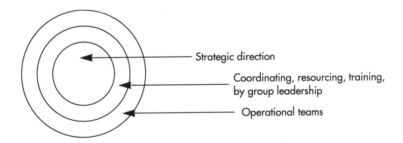

This envisages new skills, new behaviours, incorporating earning skill based pay increases geared to cross-training (multi-skilling).

It is not a panacea to an organisation in the doldrums, to be administered as a nostrum. It must be a sustained commitment from top management downwards and the successful implementation will take time and effort.

Team building is not always appropriate — there must be a group of people with common job goals which they can reach better by working together than by working individually. They must be mutually dependent on each other's experience and ability and be able to share a commitment to task achievement. Furthermore, the organisation culture must be such that managers are prepared to relinquish much of their traditional authority and be prepared to take on new roles of guiding, coaching and support — and this will not happen overnight. Many are reluctant to lose conferred power.

Yet organisations which genuinely have made this turnaround are now seen as market leaders in their various fields. Many CEOs see this development as an essential step towards enterprise survival and growth. In many cases designations have been changed — from supervisor to team leader and from manager to group leader.

If there is to be team work there are prerequisites
— there must be a stability and a compatability in the team. A group of temporary workers is not a team. Changing membership in a group means that the supervisor is constantly seeking to build a team but may only achieve elements of it
— the organisation must be committed to the concept of team work and all managers must be fully supportive in its implementation. Training plans to this end must be in place and budget provision be made.

The commitment must be genuine and sustained. There can be difficulties initially here for there may already be practices in place which emphasise recognition of the individual and do not recognise the importance of team effort. For instance

- Performance management which assigns accountability to the individual and rewards achievement on this basis
- Individual contracts of employment which require predetermined outcomes
- Career planning geared to personal training programmes
- Individual appraisal processes.

Yet team development may be the key ingredient which will give you the competitive edge in the marketplace. You should discuss with management what incentives could be generated to encourage and support the team contribution. It may take a year or more to bring this to fruition. Regular team performance appraisal should be introduced.

**So, where do you start?**

The first step is to know why your work group, your team, was established, what part it plays in the enterprise and what its future role is likely to be. With this knowledge you should then build up a picture of what, under the right conditions, it could do under your leadership. This is your vision. If you don't have this nothing will happen.

The next step is to convert this vision into a beacon, something tangible which your people can see and then follow because it makes sense and they want to. A staff meeting is a good launching pad. The key is communication. The pattern of such a meeting might be
— discussing the organisation mission statement and how it relates to what the unit actually does

166

— from this the group should compile its own Team Mission statement — challenging and meaningful. (In a large garage the mechanics put up a sign reading 'We repair cars. We have no dissatisfied customers' and the team pride was such that any incompetent or non-co-operative mechanic was quickly forced out)
— list everything that members feel could impact on this goal and inhibit its accomplishment (brainstorming would help here)
— identify the key factors for team success (KFS) — 'We must . . .' or 'We need . . .'. If possible these should be limited to seven
— prioritise these
— encourage the team to set objectives, to prepare action plans and performance standards — and to take group and individual responsibility for finding solutions
— plan follow-up meetings.

If this sequence is agreed and the follow-up is maintained team building is taking shape.

As it develops a team is likely to go through a series of formative stages

1  Initially people will tend to keep their feelings hidden, to go with the flow, to look to the appointed leader, not to listen to each other, and to be apprehensive of change. Training commences in the functioning of teams, in communication, problem solving, conflict resolution, and control techniques.
2  Relationships become more important, cliques form, the leadership is evaluated, team needs are identified, individual strengths and weaknesses become known.
3  More willingness to experiment, ways of doing things are examined, values and assumptions are discussed, more participation from those who earlier had held back, the team begins to deal with difficulties, multi-skilling continues.
4  Team pride emerges, problem solving is sought, objectives are clear and target achievement is important, the team has a protective identity, it begins to exercise its own discipline and to be more conscious of the wider environment.
5  Maturity. Leadership is decided by the situation, individual needs are recognised and met, conflicts are resolved, inter-team relationships are strengthened. Targets are met cost-effectively, activities are reviewed systematically.

But within the team individual differences are important. Each has a role to play which is based on their customary social behaviours. Some are

• **Organisers** — shaping the way the team works, focusing on real issues and targets, and seeking to impose a pattern on events.

- **Team members** — the worker bee, conscientious, hard working, seeks harmony and conformity.
- **Innovators** — seeking to test the limits of the possible, the non-conformist explorer of ideas, seeing the big picture, tending to be impatient of details.
- **Detailers** — concerned with by-the-book actions and with dotting 'i's' and crossing 't's'. Unhappy with risk and uncertainty, and hate loose ends.
- **Critics** — concerned with consequences, with what 'they' will think and may do, will choose 'safe' options.
- **Leaders** — have vision about direction and focus, and a skill in gaining the commitment of others to achieve it. Concerned with coordination of activities and with individual and team development.

Many people are a mix of these roles, some may have distinctive characteristics. A well-balanced team will have appropriate representation — and the team should be aware of the need for this. In one organisation a team of managers was concerned to find that in their membership they lacked any innovative skills. Training in creative thinking became a high priority.

Managers need to be aware of the significance of this in the context of their expectations of team output, for supervisors are not often able to determine the make-up of their teams.

As a supervisor, if the nature of your work has discretionary components the need for a balanced input is critical and if any of the above qualities are lacking you should make your team aware of the deficiency and seek to develop it.

A team will tend to resist outside intervention. Members will seek ownership of the conditions under which they work. Controls come under this heading and are likely to be given more attention if, for instance, the team is asked to consider 'in the work we do, and with regard to all cost factors, how can our performance be measured most effectively?'

This raises a significant point which supervisors must recognise. Strong teams can become competitive with each other, or become focused on their own exclusivity — and in either case the organisation is the loser.

**Within the organisation there must be coordination and co-operation — competition is expressed in the marketplace.**

Team building and team maintenance requires your unremitting attention. A team which demonstrates commitment will

- Consistently achieve targets
- Be concerned with

quality management
customer focus
continuous improvement
cost-effectiveness
competitive advantage
- Develop people for more responsible positions and inculcate leadership qualities.

Teams will demand lots of measurements of their outputs and lots of feedback. They want to know at all times how they are doing relative to targets. In a winning team

- The team has clear objectives and accepts the standards which must be met
- The team is well led and good leadership skills are demonstrated
- Individuals are competent and are multi-skilled in performing required tasks. Co-operation is taken for granted and there is mutual support and trust
- The team monitors its own performance and manages its own budget and resources
- Members know how their work relates to that of other teams and to customer/client expectation, and coordination of activity is continuous
- There is effective two-way communication throughout the organisation and constant feedback on progress towards target achievement
- The team responds to challenges, self-growth and direction is encouraged
- The team is consulted in decision making whenever appropriate and members are trained in problem-solving techniques
- Group and individual training and coaching is continuous
- There is constant seeking for improvement and change is seen as growth rather than threat. The atmosphere is informal but dynamic.

169

> How does your unit measure up?
> Discussing these questions at a staff meeting and following up the points emerging could be very productive. A similar discussion with your manager could also be useful.

## LEADERSHIP

Leader: A person who guides or inspires others.
Manager: A person who directs or manages an activity.

These definitions suggest that as required by the situation at any time a supervisor must be competent to fill both roles. The latter is backed by the authority conferred on the position. The former is dependent upon the vision and the influence of the individual and upon the sustained support of those influenced. Neither position can exist without the voluntary commitment of those being led or managed.

There are many definitions of leadership

— the ability to persuade others to seek certain goals and the skill of taking them there
— influencing the behaviour of individuals and the group towards a desired result
— the ability to convert a vision into a beacon that people follow because they want to
— 'of the best leaders, when their task is accomplished and their work is done the people will say "we did it ourselves"' (Lao Tsu).
— shaping and sharing a vision which gives purpose to the work of others
— 'Leadership is the human factor that binds a group together and motivates it towards goals. A good leader plans work, organises the group, and makes decisions — but in the final analysis none of these things get results. Planning, organising and decision making are dormant until the leader triggers the power of motivation in people and guides them towards goals. Leadership transfers potential into reality. It is the ultimate act which brings to success all the potential in an organisation and in its people.'

(Source unknown)

But to put it into the reality of the supervisor's job — you can buy people's time, you can buy their involvement in doing work — but the agreed rates of pay make no provision for enthusiasm, for team pride, for loyalty. The average person is prepared to give these freely in return for evidence that he or she really counts for something and that the job done has value and is appreciated.

Market place recognition and survival will depend upon this extra effort at all levels.
Leadership is concerned with
(a) **the tasks to be done**

• defining the objective
• planning how to proceed
• allocating work and using resources
• controlling performance
• maintaining customer focus and continuous improvement.

## (b) the team

- setting standards for quality, cost and output
- building a team spirit
- coaching when needed
- keeping them informed on what is happening or is going to happen
- encouraging self-direction and self-discipline within the group.

## (c) the individuals who make up the team

- recognising and developing individual abilities
- individual training
- encouraging and empowering growth.

## (d) the environment:

- meeting the environmental need where appropriate — what the community agrees is necessary and acceptable.

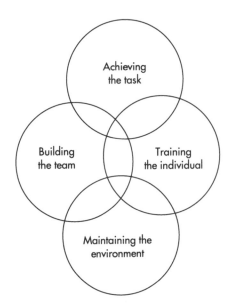

People need to feel an ownership in what they are doing.

But being a leader in the work place is not easy. It's not just a matter of following a formula. It is more likely to be the dilemma of balancing priorities. If the drive for profitability is dominant, if very tight deadlines must be met, if nothing matters but bottom line imperatives then these are the priorities for the supervisor. Under these conditions there is a real danger that concern for people becomes secondary and it can be overlooked that **the stronger and more competent the work team the better is the chance of achieving targets**.

On the other hand, if the organisation has a particularly strong social orientation the emphasis will be on concern for people perhaps to the extent that effort will be directed more into 'providing fish instead of teaching people how to fish'.

Work place leadership requires a blending and a combination of many qualities — including persuading, facilitating and empowering — but the associated management elements must include direction and control. Even if the supervisor is now called team leader there remains personal accountability for performance and outcome.

Accountability cannot be assigned to a group — it would be unenforceable. By whichever title or whatever method someone is appointed to get work done through the work of others and that is the sole reason for such appointment. This will require, when appropriate, the exercise of authority.

But as already discussed the best results are achieved only by people who believe in what they are doing and who are committed to its success, sometimes in a highly competitive environment.

**Management can provide the structure, the standards, all the resources — but only leadership can make it happen.** Motivation cannot be mandated.

The concern for results must be matched with a concern for people.

Where would you place yourself in the following grid?

| Concern for people | |
| --- | --- |
| • High concern for people<br>• Lower priorities for bottom line imperatives | • High concern for people<br>• High concern for results |
| • Less concern for people<br>• More concerned with the status quo than objectives | • High concern for results<br>• Less concern for people |

Concern for achieving objectives

Your leadership ability will be determined by the **knowledge** you have of your job and its place in the total activity, your supervisory **skills**, and the **attitudes, philosophy** and **beliefs** you have towards people at work and the things that make them tick, and towards your work objectives.

Leadership can be learned but it needs considerable self-direction and a receptiveness to new ideas.

Perhaps an initiating trigger might be to set a task: '**to improve productivity by utilising people's creativity and effort as well as their**

**hands.**' This would require recognising that output targets, meeting standards and budget, and the utilisation of resources cost-effectively are all factors imposed from external sources. The only really unique contribution a supervisor can make is to manage and lead his/her team to develop and produce everyone's best efforts. Perhaps the assessment of supervisory effectiveness is then to ask

'Did you achieve the task?

develop the individual?

build the team?

further the interests of the organisation?'

What if that were to be the basis of Supervisory Performance appraisal?

Are there identifications of leadership? The research on this would fill a Library but common findings assert that a leader

- Directs energy into accomplishing goals
- Leads by action and example
- Is prepared to seize opportunities and to take justifiable risk
- Is willing to share power and to develop leadership in others
- Builds and empowers a multi-skilled team
- Does both short and long-term planning
- Takes care to build networks and to learn from benchmarking
- Continuously looks for learning opportunities
- Is concerned with the growth both of the individual and the team and of the wider organisation
- Has good conceptual skills.

173

In today's organisations managers have to learn to think like leaders, and supervisors who wish to be seen as leaders will

- Set group goals with members of the team
- Help them to reach these goals
- Coordinate the activities to get the best from each person
- Help each individual to become a part of the team
- Seek the continuing success of the team in achieving objectives
- Demonstrate good human relations
- Use power wisely
- Convey a sense of purpose
- Know when to take a hands-off stance.

## LEADING CHANGE

Change is the process by which the future invades our lives. Change is inevitable. Everything either improves, deteriorates or undergoes change, and in today's technology most of our working processes are changing. Yet people tend to resist change. In a familiar setting they feel secure and comfortable, and change can produce dislocation, instability and anxiety. Some liken change to a comet — a shining front and a long tail full of debris.

As a supervisor you will have to introduce and lead change. To avoid any disruption you will have to be sure that your team recognises that the change is needed and that the proposed change is the right change. This will require advance discussion with them to reassure them regarding the expected effects of the change and to seek their support and co-operation in introducing it.

An instinctive response to change is 'What's in it for me?' and the answer to this has to be convincing.

Resistance can be triggered by many fears, e.g. fear of
    redundancy
    loss of security
    disorganisation
    loss of status
    inability to cope
    loss of existing relationships, etc.

or by general apathy or a feeling of denial of existing expectations — the reasons are many.

People usually co-operate if they feel they will
    gain benefit, or
    avoid loss
and without acceptable responses to their uncertainties they will resist change sometimes even to the point of sabotaging it.

The advantages of the change should be seen to outweigh the disadvantages.

Your hand should move the lever of change towards growth.

One approach to leading change is to
— identify the required outcome of the change
— discuss the change with those who will be involved
— analyse and plan the change procedures
— gain acceptance of the proposed change
— check the step by step introduction of the change to ensure that it proceeds as planned
— follow up to ensure that what was intended has, in fact, been achieved.

With your team you should, if time permits, prepare a timetable for a trial run or a pilot effort to precede the final installation.

174

The following factors will ensure successful implementation

— the organisation feels it is its own project and not one devised and operated by outsiders
— the project has top-level commitment and support
— the change is seen as improving the work situation or reducing the present work pressures
— the project accords with values and ideals which are acknowledged by the participants
— the programme offers a new experience which will interest the participants
— the participants feel that their present autonomy and security is not threatened
— the participants have been consulted or involved in diagnostic efforts leading them to agree on what the basic problem is and to feel its importance
— the project is adopted by consensual group decision
— the proponents are able to confer and discuss with opponents; to recognise valid objections; and to take steps to relieve unnecessary fears
— it is recognised that innovations are likely to be misunderstood and misinterpreted, and provision is made for feedback of perceptions of the project and for further clarification as needed
— participants experience acceptance, support, trust and confidence in their relations with one another
— the project is kept open to revision and reconsideration if experience indicates that changes would be desirable.

175

**The keystone of leading change is consultation — but there must be a person in the driving seat and a source of power.**

What are the roadblocks that keep your people from contributing more to productive change? What needs to be done?

Careful planning is a prerequisite of effective change. Options and their likely consequences must be studied — but there will always be a measure of risk. Unknown factors will inevitably surface. What happened in the past is seldom an accurate forecaster of tomorrow's events — and you cannot lead your team into change while looking in to the rearview mirror.

You move forward with confidence, and with some contingency plans.

So, what can go wrong? Anything and everything. For instance

• The impact of external events, e.g.
  — financial or trading fluctuations

  — political decisions
  — competitor actions
- Inadequate provision for dealing with consequences
- Passive acceptance of the change did not create a commitment to carry it out
- A willingness to backtrack when opposition appears (implying a lack of belief in the change action) instead of consultation or negotiation or decision to continue on the agreed course. A lack of planning and of leadership
- Unclear definition of the change processes, details overlooked
- Accountability for outcomes not assigned
- Time pressures.

The time factor can be a major cause of concern. Once a need for change has been perceived the desired sequence of action could be described as:

| Awareness | Interest | Planning | Pilot project | Evaluation | Adoption of change | Review |

Today that reflective process would be the rare exception. Change is happening so quickly and is being forced by so many factors that often there is quite inadequate time for consultation, there is no pilot project, and before implementation has settled down a need for further change has appeared. The sequence has become:

Awareness          Decide response          Take action

Change is now the only constant.
  Which means that you must seek from management the maximum advance notice of pending change so that your team can be prepared. Recent events in many areas show a decrease in trust between management and employees. The statement 'They don't need to know that yet' has done much to foul up the smooth impact of change. And the resultant resentment has damaged effective team output.

Introduction                                    New challenges
  Opposition                                  Commitment
    Rejection                                Adoption
      Obstruction                          Identification
        Explanation                      Acceptance
          Discussion                  Understanding

How long does it take your organisation to work through the attitude to change cycle?

It is a test of culture and of leadership.

> You may find it useful to have a checklist.
> What is the change?
> What is its real objective?
> When will it happen?
> What will be the effects — now?
>            later?
> Who will it involve?
> What may or will it do to them?
> Is there sufficient lead time for consultation?
> What is the best way of dealing with it?
> What other options are there?
> Can we trial any of it?
> How else can we underwrite its acceptance?
> How will success be demonstrated?

177

The criteria for success are

- Was it generally accepted?
- Was it implemented in accordance with the plan?
- Was the cost close to budget?
- Is whatever has changed now performing as it was meant to?
- What specific observable outcomes have emerged?
- What is the reaction of those involved?

> - In your organisation what changes do you expect to occur during, say, the next 18 months?
> - List the people who will be affected, directly and indirectly. How well prepared are they now?
> - What steps will you need to take to manage each change effectively?

# PART 4

# SELF-DIRECTION

## CHAPTER 10

# SELF-DIRECTION

In your reflection on the elements of this chapter think, too, about the importance of
    self-knowledge
    self-management
    self-development
It's your future

## WHERE ARE YOU NOW?

If you're not prepared to invest in your own future why should anyone else?

Perhaps a good place to start is to identify the positive factors you currently have, and there are many.

### As an individual you have

- Education
- Experience
- Physical abilities
- Mental abilities
- Income
- Time
- Family
- Capacity for friendship
- Capacity for relationships
- Opportunity for initiative

### As a supervisor you have

- Management support
- Responsibility and authority
- Work schedules and projects
- People
- A budget and other resources
- Work layout
- Work flow
- Time
- Networks
- Opportunity for initiative

Consider each of these — what more could you be doing with what you have? What's stopping you?

Accepting that behaviour is everything you say and do, only you can choose how you behave. Ralph Waldo Emerson, the American essayist, said 'The power which resides in you is new in nature, and none but you knows what that is which you can do, nor do you know until you have tried.'

182

YOU are the centre of your world.

Each of us is.

Yet we cannot exist alone. We are surrounded by others with whom we have relationships of varying closeness. Some we are very close to now, with some we would like to be closer, with others there is a distance between us.

Write in below the names of those with whom you associate, showing how close you feel them to be today. Then draw arrows to show how close you would like them to be.

It's your world. Perhaps this means that it's your responsibility to take the initiatives. Where do you think you are within each of their circles?

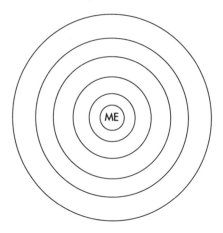

And to continue with this analysis of where you are now, rate yourself on a 10-point scale (10 high) on your people skills and your task skills.

Your people skills

- Communicating clearly and listening
- Developing, training and coaching
- Gaining social acceptance
- Gaining commitment of individuals and the group
- Sharing forecasts and feedback
- People problem solving
- Recognising performance achievement
- Leading a winning team
- Gaining acceptance as one of the management team
- Building networks.

Your task skills

- Achieving targets within budget
- Maintaining quality standards and customer focus
- Acting proactively
- Seeking continuous improvement
- Analytical problem solving
- Responding to challenge
- Accepting responsibility and accountability
- Concern for cost-effectiveness of effort
- In-house coordination and co-operation
- Contribution to the organisation's business plan.

183

If you plot your ratings on a graph you have probably created an agenda for action, and some priorities may emerge.

But there is one critical factor here. You have a work life and many responsibilities. You have a personal life and many responsibilities. Are they in balance?

Work                    Personal

If you have a breakdown due to overwork or to work stress, who in the organisation is really going to care? When looking at an organisation one might ask about

- Why it exists — its purpose — its ideology
- Its vision — what it needs to do to achieve its purpose — its philosophy
- Its strategy — how to implement its plans and use its technology.

Doesn't this apply equally to making a living and to planning how to live?

Aim to work smarter, to do better — and this shouldn't mean working longer hours. Some pressure is necessary for effective living, but pace yourself so that the stress is tolerable and perhaps even exciting. When the tension builds, as it will occasionally, take time out for a few minutes and consider

- are my priorities right?
- have I explored all my options?
- if I weren't here what would happen?
- what's the real bottom line on this?

To quote two unknown writers
'There's no such thing as darkness, only a failure to see.'

and

'Fear is the darkroom in which negatives are developed.'


## WHERE DO YOU WANT TO BE?

Your promotion and your development are mainly a matter of self-development. The organisation should provide training and the opportunity for development — but the drive, the desire, the effort, the obligation, and the responsibility for growth rests with you.

184

Hard work by itself is seldom the only way to promotion. You should prepare for the job ahead. Critically seek to identify the skills and the knowledge that you lack, and then set out to master them. And, at the same time, train someone to be ready to take over your job.

At least once a year you should have a full and frank discussion with your manager and ask, 'How am I getting on?' 'How can I do better?' And regularly you should do a personal stocktaking and then plan to take action on what you feel needs improving.

A start point for this is to go through each of the items on your Job Description and to see whether or not you are meeting fully the objectives they cover. There may be some things you really haven't got to grips with — perhaps because you haven't been trained to do them, or because you don't like doing them. How important are they? Could your weakness here be delaying a promotion? In this review of your own ability you should be quite ruthless with yourself.

Once you have identified an area for self-improvement you should prepare a specific action plan and a target date, e.g. 'by .................. (date) I will be able to ............................................ and my competence will be demonstrated by ........................'

The first step towards self-improvement is to know what needs to be improved. The second step is to do something about it.

- Consider undertaking a study course leading to a recognised qualification (certificate, diploma, or degree)
- Ask to be sent to appropriate training courses
- Ask your manager for a recommended reading list.

You should also look wider. Organisations rise and fall. Few stay the same. Today people tend to change jobs several times during their working lives. Is your present job set in a fairly restricted field or do you have a lot of variety and discretion? In either case are you building a balance of skills? There are four areas in which you should demonstrate competence

- Technical
- People
- Finance
- Marketing.

**Elements for my success**

| Technical | People | Finance | Marketing |
|---|---|---|---|
| My knowledge and skill are the key to my position | People and money are my major resources — I need to be able to use the optimum facilities of both | | I am dependent upon meeting the needs and expectations of others |
| • Why was my job established?<br>• What is the perceived bottom line? does this limit or challenge me?<br>• How well am I really performing?<br>• Where do I need to improve now? what am I doing about it?<br>• What am I/should I be doing to update my technical knowledge and skill? update my managerial knowledge and skill? | • What are the strengths and weaknesses of my people skills?<br>• How effective am I as a team leader, or a team member?<br>• Whom do I depend on? why?<br>• Who depends on me? what for?<br>• Who influences me? how? is this good or bad?<br>• Whom do I influence? why? how?<br>• What do I need to do to optimise these things? | • Where does my job fit in the financial plan for this unit?<br>• Do I really understand our financial records and analyses and our unit's involvement in them?<br>• I am a cost centre what are the direct and indirect costs of my position? what are the financial expectations of my output?<br>• What are the components of our budget? how do I/could I influence this?<br>• What more could be done within that budget? | • Who are my customers/clients?<br>• What are their special needs? how do I know?<br>• How am I responding to these needs? with what success? what else should/ could I do?<br>• What changes are likely in any of these areas? what must I do to cope?<br>• Is my marketing plan reviewed regularly? |

185

## PRESENTATION SKILLS

Many supervisors — and many managers — are not promoted because they lack presentation skills.

These can include the ability to

- talk to a group of people
- present a case to management
- influence a group of people
- chair a meeting
- write and present a report
- deal with correspondence by draft or dictation
- use basic statistical data
- be computer literate
- be interviewed by the media press and TV
- relate freely and effectively with people of other cultures and ethnic origins
- lead a training session.

186

Obviously you won't have to do all of these things, but can you identify with certainty the ones which you won't have to do within the next two years?

Some good practical books and a range of training courses and videos are now available and can give a grounding in the basics — but as you know you can't learn by correspondence how to ride a bicycle. Seize opportunities to do these things and ask someone with experience to comment and give helpful hints. Clubs like Toastmasters can be most supportive.

Competency in presentation skills will give a major boost to self-confidence, enhance your leadership image and thereby your promotion potential.

## BUILDING YOUR NETWORK

In some situations whom you know can be as important as what you know.

Who has information you want? Who has already had to deal with a problem now facing you? Who can give you completely independent advice? What impact will new technology have in your field of activity in the next three years? Who are your opposite numbers in other similar organisations — here and overseas? Who do you contact at outside meetings?

You should develop and maintain a network of names, designations, addresses, contact numbers, etc. of people who can or could be helpful in a wide variety of ways — held either in an indexed notebook or by a simple filing of business cards.

Networking can be significantly useful in your own effectiveness and growth. You should try and extend it each month.

## GAIN QUALIFICATION

Qualifications may well become important planks in building your success platform. Acquisition is evidence of a trained mind even if the qualification itself is not wholly relevant to the tasks being performed.

It is becoming accepted that no formal training course should be a dead end. From this experience you should be able to step up to another level of progression (This is known as **staircasing** or **articulation**).

This was illustrated earlier. By drawing on the skills experience you have accumulated so far, perhaps recording this in a Work Experience Log Book, and claiming recognition of your prior learning, you may already be able to obtain some exemptions or credits towards an established qualification.

Staircasing such as this could offer second-chance education with a ceiling limited only by the ability and determination of the individual.

187

Its potential is a challenge to all who design staff development activity.

### A Project

1  List at least 4 problem areas or difficulties which are causing you concern at work.
2  Rank them in a priority and deal with them in this sequence.
3  Explore 'Why?' and 'How?' did this situation develop.
4  Identify all the options for resolving it satisfactorily. Select the best.
5  Prepare an Action Plan. Nominate a target date.
6  Outline clearly the conditions which will apply when your objective is achieved.
7  Before doing anything discuss your outline with a colleague to test its validity.

## HOW TO MANAGE YOUR BOSS

This is not about a power struggle or seeking to win a difficult battle, for anyone with experience in 'street smarts' or 'living in the organisation jungle' will know that the first law of survival is **make your boss look good**.

You and your boss should be in partnership for you share the same objectives. But each of you has a different personality, different behavioural responses, and probably different strengths and weaknesses. Therefore, you should try to identify, by observation and discussion, what these differences are, so that as and when appropriate you may reinforce each other.

| Your boss may have | You may have |
|---|---|
| • A wider view and knowledge of the situation | • More detailed knowledge of the work place realities |
| • More command of resources | • Understanding of people's abilities to use them |
| • More experience and product or service knowledge | • More awareness of customer needs and responses |
| • An enthusiasm for more, better, cheaper, faster | • A realisation of individual, group and time limitations |
| • A feeling of isolation | • Team support |

You should use the approach 'From where I sit and with the knowledge I have this is how I see it . . ., but if you don't see it the same way may we discuss it?' Collaboration not confrontation.

Find out how he/she likes to delegate — seldom, often, in broad outline or detailed — and show your competence in your performance.

Don't go in with problems, go in with recommendations.

Find out how your boss prefers to operate, e.g.

— risk taker, innovative, conservative
— quick or slow decision maker
— seeks or avoids conflict
— good or poor organiser of time and work
— delegates or abdicates
— wants information orally or in writing
— how seen by peers and management
— autocratic or democratic leadership
— breadth of vision.

You are dependent on each other for your success and by understanding your separate styles, building rapport so that you may discuss them, you will soon see the most effective ways of working together and helping each other with complementary skills.

But you must be aware of the danger of by-passing. If your boss gives instructions directly to members of your unit this must be stopped (unless it is warranted by special circumstances). You should say 'When you go directly to them they are confused — do they then report directly back to you or to me? And if to you you must realise that I can no longer be held accountable for setting and maintaining work flow priorities. If my people see uncertainty here they will find ways of playing us off against each other.' Don't let by-passing continue; it is a major fault in many organisations.

Your boss depends on you to achieve targets by the sustained performance of your team. That gives you power. And it is in his/her interests to support and coach you for the results will enhance both your reputations. Therefore, your harmonious relationship becomes a critical factor.

189

# CHAPTER 11

# IN SUMMARY

To be effective in your job you must be able to:

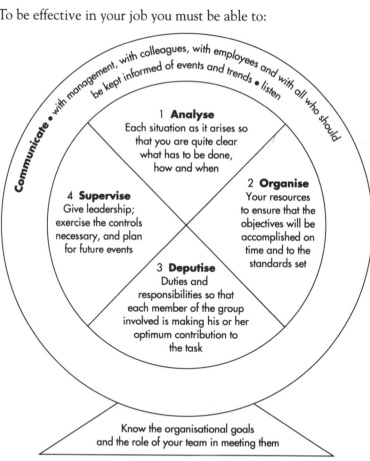

Communicate • with management, with colleagues, with employees and with all who should be kept informed of events and trends • listen

**1 Analyse**
Each situation as it arises so that you are quite clear what has to be done, how and when

**2 Organise**
Your resources to ensure that the objectives will be accomplished on time and to the standards set

**3 Deputise**
Duties and responsibilities so that each member of the group involved is making his or her optimum contribution to the task

**4 Supervise**
Give leadership; exercise the controls necessary, and plan for future events

Know the organisational goals and the role of your team in meeting them

And in doing these things

| You should | You should not |
|---|---|
| Know your objectives and know how they fit in with other activities | Be concerned just with the routine activities of your unit and ignore everything else |
| Make it clear to your team what is expected<br>    what output is required<br>    the standards set<br>    possible problems | Keep people in the dark yet still expect good results<br><br>Overload the willing or the weak<br><br>Expect the same from everyone |
| Allocate work fairly, having regard to people's abilities | Leave them in doubt |
| Give credit and constructive criticism in your coaching | Reprimand in the presence of others |
| Guide and explain | Bluster |
| Be reliable, consistent and dependable | Neglect promises |
| Listen | Just talk at them |
| Exercise controls fairly and without favour | Condone or ignore poor performance or inadequate results |
| Show confidence in people and be available to them if needed | Underestimate the capacity of your people<br><br>Breathe down their necks |
| Try to help each person develop his or her potential and to grow in the job | Be content just with producing the work expected from the group |
| Achieve targets | |

191

**The Task**

**Mission**
Financially viable
Future conscious

Market directed
Results oriented

**Functions**
Strategic planning
Objective setting
Tactical planning
Action
Performance measurement
Coordination
Resource management
Benchmarking
Networking

**Goal achievement**

**Train to develop competency**
For today
For tomorrow
Accept ownership
of objectives

2

**Team building**
Developing synergy
Concern to match
product or service
with customers'
expectations

3

**Selection and introduction**
Sharing the vision

1

**Innovation**
Concern for quality
— to achieve better with less

4

**Growth**
Reinforcing
and extending
the competitive edge

5

**People**
Contributing and empowered
Seeking responsibility
Self-developing

Trained — keen to learn
Informed and sharing
Committed to targets

**Requisites**
Participatively led
Shared objectives
Quality motivated
Continuous improvement
Unclogged communication
Cost conscious
Assigned accountability
Competency qualified

A personal check list:

> **Better supervision**
> Do I know quite clearly what is my objective?
> Are there standards by which I may measure performance?
> Do I have the necessary resources?
> Am I working to a defined plan? Are the controls appropriate?
> Do I know regularly how well I am progressing?
> Am I getting the right results? (quality, quantity, cost, time.)
> Have I established clear lines of direct responsibility and authority?
> Am I doing work which should be delegated?
> Am I making good decisions?
> Am I meeting my responsibilities for training and coaching?
> Is my communication really effective? Do I listen?
> Do all my subordinates fully understand their individual roles and
>     objectives? Are they committed to their achievement?
> Am I giving credit for good work?
> How well do we work as a team?
>
> ───────────────
>
> How would each of my staff answer these questions? How do I know?
> Where should I be seeking improvement?

193

As someone once said: 'If only I were half as good a supervisor as I know how to be, I would be superb.'

*'To be what we are and to become what we are capable of becoming is the only end of life.'*

# A GLOSSARY OF MANAGEMENT TERMS

**Accountability:** Liability for results. It is the next step after responsibility.

**Authority:** The power assigned to take action.

**Benchmarking:** The process of exploring the competitive market, nationally and internationally to identify the best practice in a product, process or service, and to gain from this analysis.

**Best practice:** The creation of a standard of performance emerging from benchmarking, nationally and internationally, and from in-house quality management, which combine to give superior output at the time.

**Communication:** Transfer of meaning from one mind to another. The outcome, the reception, is the communication — not the transmission. Listening is an active process, requiring hearing, evaluating, interpreting and reacting.

**Competency:** The acquisition of specified knowledge, skills and attitudes and the application of those attributes within an occupational or industry level to the standard of performance required and assessed by the employer.

**Culture:** The organisational values, norms and beliefs which will influence what happens. The reasons why people are promoted will sometimes reveal this.

**Delegation:** To entrust part of one's authority to another whilst retaining responsibility for the exercise of that authority.

**Empathy:** The ability to sense the inner world of other people and to understand how they feel.

**Empowerment:** Helping supervisors take ownership of their own jobs so that they take personal interest in improving team performance supporting team members and achieving organisational targets.

**KFS:** Key Factors for Success — the critical components of strategic and tactical planning.

**KPI:** Key Performance Indicators are results that measure the effectiveness of an organisation or individual.

**KRA:** Key Results Areas — synonymous terms for defining specific areas of accountability of an individual or group.

**Leadership:** Shaping and sharing a vision which gives purpose and commitment to the work of others.

**Line and staff:** Line people are operational employees concerned with meeting the functional requirements of the enterprise. Their positions carry both responsibility and authority. Staff people fill advisory or helping roles in which they carry responsibility but not authority. Their tasks end with recommendations to line management and their power is dependent upon their influence.

**Manager:** A senior in-charge position. One to whom supervisors report. The primary task is to achieve objectives through leadership by the use of objective setting, planning, action and control techniques.

**Managing diversity:** Recognising that people have differing abilities and potential, and training and developing them accordingly. As opposed to managing conformity.

**Marketing:** The combination of skills, decisions and activities required in identifying, anticipating and satisfying the customer's needs and desires. Selling is concerned with persuasion.

**Mindmap:** A diagram to present ideas and information on a particular subject in a creative mode. Related to brainstorming.

**Mission statement:** A statement of intent which describes for all to see the organisational or unit purpose and direction.

**Morale:** Confidence in the organisation

**Motivation:** The internalised drive towards the dominant thought of the moment. You can't motivate anyone — you can only create a situation to which he or she will respond.

**Networking:** The establishment of relationships with individuals or groups of people with the objective of information sharing, enhancing work and personal life.

**Organisation:** A network of relationships between people working together for a common purpose. Communication is the fabric of it.
*Formal* organisation, the area of authority, defines the visible shape, structure, policy, rules, regulations and procedures of the enterprise.
*Informal* organisation, the unseen area of influence, is more concerned with the social groups, behavioural patterns, beliefs and objectives and personality power. Organisational politics are based on the interactions within this, and the use of its communication network, the grapevine.

**Performance management:** A system of job evaluation, individually agreed objective setting, coaching and regular appraisal of objective achievement geared to salary recognition. The principle is based on payment for results rather than payment based on other criteria. Each organisation must structure its own gestation period for this to ensure that the implementation will have wholly positive outcomes.

**Planning:** The thinking that precedes the doing; for instance, what is the task? what results are expected? what is the best way to do it? It must involve the future, people and action and combine facts and imagination.

*Strategic* planning is concerned with organisational objectives, the resources needed to achieve the objectives, and the policies that govern the acquisition, use and disposition of those resources.

*Tactical* planning defines the tactics and procedures for converting the strategic plan into reality.

**Power:** The ability or the capacity to do something — the ability to control. It can stem from many sources — status, assigned, personality, competence, alliances — and can be demonstrated at all levels. If peer pressure is the strongest motivator and a major power source how does a leader exercise countervailing power?

**QM:** Quality Management: all those planned and systematic actions necessary to provide adequate confidence that a product or service will satisfy given requirements for quality. It aims at reducing waste and improving competitiveness.

**Quality:** The presence of value and fitness for use as perceived by the customer. Cost-effective defect free action meeting the full requirements of the customer now and in the future.

**Quality assurance:** Systems for measuring production set against criteria, using quality tools to a specific end.

**Quality improvement:** A broader concept incorporating a range of management techniques covering all elements of the operations. It is people focused.

**Recognition of Prior Learning (RPL):** The assessment of competencies gained from previous experiences, then using this as a launching pad to acquire new learning.

**Responsibility:** A requirement to take action.

**Skills:** Acquired ability as a result of learning and practice.

**Span of control:** The maximum number of people reporting directly to one controlling officer. There is no defined maximum number. It will depend upon the nature of the work and the skill of those doing it.

**Stress:** The tension which results when your cope runneth over.

**Supervisor:** The first level in-charge position with hands on control of getting work done by others to meet defined targets. Supervisors play a significant role in the pursuit of effectiveness and profitability.

**Task:** A defined element of work.

**Teams:** Cohesive work groups which are given and develop defined responsibilities of their daily activities.

**Time Based Competition (TBC):** A work flow process aiming to eliminate waste at any stage of activities to maximise the proportion of time available to add value to the product or service.

**Total Quality Management (TQM):** Incorporates Quality Assurance, Quality Improvement and Statistical Process Control (QA + Q1 + SPC), and requires total organisational commitment operationally led by managers and supervisors. The international standards association has published a series of standards (The ISO 9000 series) through which organisations who meet these standards may gain certification and accreditation.

**Unity of command:** For each task a person has to do there should be one clear point of authority. If more than one person exercises authority in the same area confusion and conflict are inevitable. This is wider than the 'one person, one boss' concept.

**Work-based learning:** A structured and integrated learning approach which incorporates off and on the job learning to meet both organisational and individual employee goals.

**Work place reform:** A concern for improving participative work practices and management styles creating quality products and services leading to enriched employee and customer satisfaction.

# INDEX

199